Azure Study & Lab Guide For Beginners

Harinder Kohli

kindle direct publishing

Contact Author

Email: harinder-kohli@outlook.com
Linkedin: www.linkedin.com/in/harinderkohli
Azure Blog @ https://mykloud.wordpress.com

TOC and Sample Chapter Download

- You can download TOC and Sample Chapter from Box.com.
- The Box.com download link is given on Amazon page from where you purchased the Book.

Contents at a Glance

Table of Contents

Chapter 1 Cloud Computing

Introduction to Server Virtualization

Before going into Cloud Computing let's discuss about Server Virtualization. Server Virtualization is the base on which Cloud Computing is built.

With Server Virtualization a hypervisor installed on compute host creates and runs Virtual Machines. Each Virtual Machine runs a unique guest operating system. VMs with different operating systems can run on the same physical server - a Windows VM can sit alongside a Linux VM.

Example of Hypervisor includes VMware ESXi, Microsoft Hyper-v, Citrix XenServer and Linux KVM.

Figure below shows architecture of Server Virtualization.

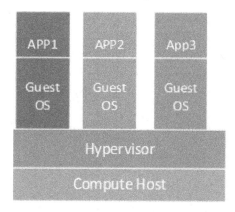

When you request a Compute instance in Azure Cloud, you don't get access to full Physical Server. Instead Automation and Orchestration technologies work in backend to create a Virtual Machine for you on a Physical Server. In Cloud this Physical Server will also host Virtual Machines for different customers.

Introduction to Cloud Computing

Cloud Computing is on-demand availability of resources such as Compute, Data Storage, Databases etc over the internet.

Cloud Computing uses Virtualization, Automation and Orchestration technologies to enable end users to use Self-service option to provision resources and deploy workloads without direct intervention from the Cloud Provider's IT staff.

With Cloud Computing, Companies rent Cloud Providers equipment using pay per use model. This reduces capital expenditure for the Companies. Cloud Providers share their equipment with Multiple Companies which allows them to price their services competitively.

Features and Benefits of Cloud Computing

Pay per use: In Pay per use model Users pay only for the time they have used the Cloud Resources.

Self-service provisioning: With Self-service option users provision compute and other resources in cloud without direct intervention from the Cloud Provider's IT staff. Secondly Companies don't require trained IT Administrators to provision cloud resources.

Scalability: You can Scale-up or Scale-down compute resources on-demand. You can Scale-up compute resources using Scale-out or Scale-up option. With Scale-out you add additional Compute Resources (Virtual Machines) to service your application. With Scale-up you use Virtual Machine with additional and more Powerful Resources. Scale-down feature helps in minimizing the cost of the compute resources in cloud.

Whereas in on-premises environment you provision compute resources as per peak requirements of the application. Peak requirement usually happens during particular time of the day or particular day in a month.

Multi-tenancy: In Public Cloud multiple customers access the same physical infrastructure. Multi-tenancy allows customers to access the same physical infrastructures and applications but they still retain privacy and security over their own data.

Cost Savings: Using cloud computing organizations reduce capital costs (Capital Expenditure or Capex) as organizations don't have to spend large amounts of money buying IT equipments and maintaining large Data Centers. Instead they pay monthly rent (Operation Expenditure or Opex) for the cloud resources they have used

High Availability and Disaster Recovery: Organizations want their Applications to be available 100% of time to avoid any Business disruption because of Application downtime. Setting up High Availability and Disaster Recovery in on-premises environment is a very expensive and time consuming process.

Public Cloud offers many features which allow you to set up High Availability and Disaster Recovery at nominal cost and time.

Using Public Cloud you can use features such as Multiple Availability Zones and Regions, Replication of Storage and Database Services within and across regions, Regional and Global Load Balancers etc to set up High Availability and Disaster Recovery quickly and at reasonable cost.

Managed Services: Managed Services is one of the main reason that organizations are moving to Cloud. Managed Services such as Database, Analytics, Big Data, Machine learning, Storage, Identity and Security does not require skilled manpower for deployment. Additional features of Managed Services such as Backup and High Availability can be configured without requiring any expertise. Managed Services can be deployed within seconds to minutes. Additionally you don't have to patch, update and upgrade Managed Services. Azure automatically patches, updates and upgrades Managed Services for you.

Cloud Computing Delivery Models

Cloud Services can be delivered in multiple ways such as IaaS, PaaS and SaaS.

The Diagram below shows the difference between IaaS, PaaS and SaaS. **The boxes with Dark grey background are managed by Cloud Provider.**

IaaS	PaaS	SaaS
Applications	Applications	Applications
Data	Data	Data
Runtime	Runtime	Runtime
Middleware	Middleware	Middleware
Operating System	Operating System	Operating System
Virtualization	Virtualization	Virtualization
Server	Server	Server
Storage	Storage	Storage
Networking	Networking	Networking

Infrastructure-as-a-Service (IaaS): IaaS refers to the Virtual Server or Virtual Machine or Compute instance offered by a Cloud Provider. End Users Install Operating System and Applications on the Compute instance. Operating System image is provided by Cloud Provider. Cloud Provider offer Multiple SKU's of Compute instance which differs in terms of CPU, Memory and Storage configurations. Examples of IaaS include AWS EC2 instance, Azure Virtual Machine and Google Compute Engine.

Platform-as-a-Service (PaaS): In PaaS model Cloud Provider delivers hardware, operating systems and Software runtime tools such as ASP.NET, PHP, Java, Node.JS, Python, Ruby etc to end users as a service. Examples of PaaS include Azure Web App, Google App Engine and AWS Elastic Beanstalk.

Software-as-a-Service (SaaS): In SaaS model Cloud Provider delivers Software Applications or Web Applications over the internet. Examples of SaaS include Salesforce CRM, Netsuite ERP and Yahoo Mail.

Cloud Computing Deployment Models

Public Cloud: In this Model Cloud Provider delivers Compute, Storage and other Cloud Services over the internet. Public Cloud uses shared infrastructure that is shared between all consumers of the public cloud. Public Cloud provides multiple benefits such as Pay per use, Scalability, Managed Services and Cost savings. Examples of Public Cloud Providers include Amazon Web Services, Google Cloud Platform and Microsoft Azure.

Private Cloud: In this Model Cloud Services are delivered through Organization owned Data Center to internal users. Private Cloud model is a Single-tenant architecture. It uses on-premises hardware and provides direct control of underlying Cloud Infrastructure. Example of Private Cloud Technologies include Openstack, Apache Cloudstack, Vmware vRealize Automation and Vmware vCloud Director.

Hybrid Cloud: Hybrid Cloud Model is a mix of on-premises infrastructure, Private Cloud and Public Cloud. In this model workloads are running in both on-premises and Public Cloud. In this Model you have multiple scenarios for running workloads. You can have Applications running in Public Cloud and they are accessing Database on-premises. You can have legacy workloads running on-premises and all other workloads running in cloud. You can have mission critical workloads running on-premises because of regulatory compliance reasons and balance workloads running in cloud.

Public Cloud Providers

Following are some of the Public Cloud Providers who offer Public Cloud Computing.

- Amazon Web Services (AWS)
- Google Cloud Platform (GCP)
- Microsoft Azure
- Oracle Cloud Infrastructure (OCI)

Chapter 2 Azure Cloud Architecture and Services

Azure Global Infrastructure consists of 2 Components: Datacenters and Network components which connect Datacenters.

Azure Datacenters

Azure Datacenters are unique physical buildings that house Racks of Computer Servers, Networking Equipments, Backup Power Supply and Generators etc.

Azure Datacenters are spread across the Globe.

Azure Regions

A region is a set of Datacenters (Availability Zones) deployed within a latency-defined perimeter and connected through a dedicated regional low-latency Fibre optic network.

Azure Region protects your applications and data from Complete Location Breakdown or Datacenter wide outage which affects the entire Availability Zone

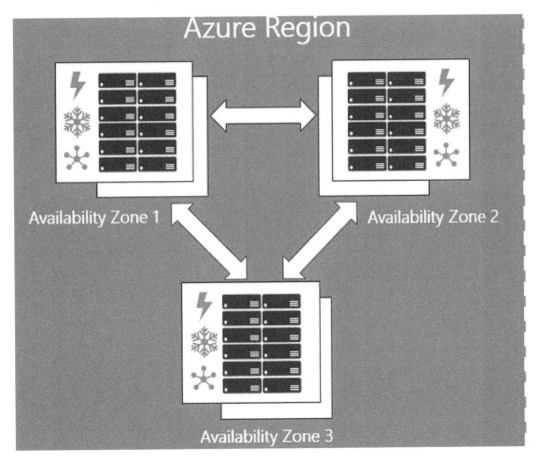

Azure Availability Zones

Azure Availability Zones are unique physical locations within an Azure region and offer high availability to protect your applications and data from Datacenter level failures. Each Availability Zone is made up of one or more Datacenters equipped with independent Power, Cooling, and Networking.

Geography

A Geography typically contains two or more regions within the same country, that preserves data residency and compliance boundaries. There are exceptions such as some Regions with EU are considered as same geography.

Geographies allow customers with specific data-residency and compliance needs to keep their data and applications close. Geographies are fault-tolerant to withstand complete region failure through their connection to dedicated high-capacity networking infrastructure.

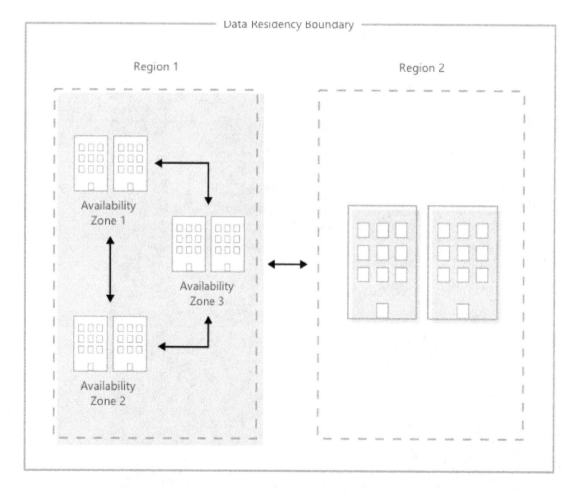

Paired Regions

Each Azure region is paired with another region within the same geography, together making a regional pair.

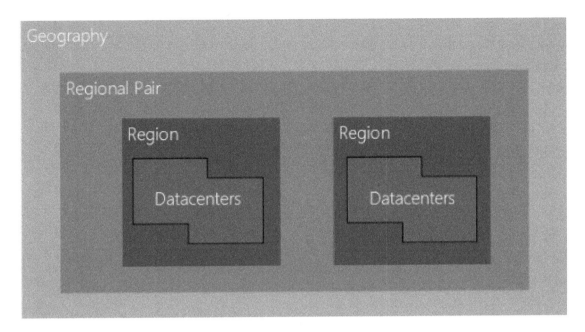

Microsoft recommends that you replicate workloads across regional pairs to benefit from Azure's isolation and availability policies. For example, planned Azure system updates are deployed sequentially (not at the same time) across paired regions. That means that even in the rare event of a faulty update, both regions will not be affected simultaneously. Furthermore, in the unlikely event of a broad outage, recovery of at least one region out of every pair is prioritized.

Table below shows some of the Azure Paired Regions.

Geography	Paired Region	Paired Region
North America	East US	West US
North America	East US 2	Central US
Canada	Canada Central	Canada East
Germany	Germany Central	Germany Northeast
India	Central India	South India
China	China North	China East
Japan	Japan East	Japan West
Korea	Korea Central	Korea South

Azure Services & Solutions

Following is partial list of Services & Solutions available in Azure Cloud.

- Virtual Machines
- Virtual Networks
- Resource Groups
- Blob Storage
- File Storage
- Azure App Service
- Azure SQL Database
- Azure Backup
- Microsoft Defender for Cloud
- Azure Monitor
- Azure Firewall
- Network Security Groups
- Virtual Network Gateway
- ExpressRoute
- Azure Kubernetes Service

In upcoming Chapter we will discuss some of the above Services & Solutions.

Chapter 3 Azure Free Trial Account and Basic Configuration

Azure Trial Account

Azure Trial Account gives you 200 Dollar credit with 30 Days validity. Remember that any balance left in your credit will expire after 30 Days.

After 30 Days convert your Azure Trial Account to Pay as you go and get access to 25+ Azure Services free for 12 Months. You can cancel your Pay as you go account any time.

Table below shows partial list of Azure Free Services available for 12 Months.

Azure Service	Type	Free Monthly Amount	Free Period
Windows VMs	Compute	750 hours B1s burstable virtual machines	12 Months
Linux VMs	Compute	750 hours B1s burstable virtual machines	12 Months
Virtual Network	Networking	50 Virtual Networks	Always
VPN Gateway	Networking	750 hours of VpnGw1 Gateway	12 Months
Azure Active Directory	Identity	50,000 stored objects with single sign-on (SSO) to all cloud apps	Always
SQL Database	Databases	250 GB S0 instance with 10 database transaction units	12 Months
Blob Storage	Storage	5 GB locally redundant storage (LRS) hot block with 20,000 read and 10,000 write operations	12 Months
Azure Kubernetes Service (AKS)	Compute	Free	Always
Bandwidth (Data Transfer)	Networking	15 GB outbound	12 Months
Bandwidth (Data Transfer)	Networking	5 GB outbound	Always
Container Registry	Containers	1 Standard tier registry with 100 GB storage and 10 webhooks	12 Months
App Service	Compute	10 web, mobile, or API apps with 1 GB storage	Always

To see the full list of free services offered for 12 Months, go to the following link.
https://azure.microsoft.com/en-us/free/

Pre-Req for creating Azure Trial Account

- Valid email-id. Make sure that this email-id was not previously used for creating Azure Trial Account. It is preferred that you use Outlook/Hotmail email account.
- Valid Mobile Number & Valid Credit Card.

Exercise 3.1: Create Azure Trial Account

1. To create Azure Trial Account go to following link: **https://signup.azure.com/**
2. Sign-in/Sign-up page opens as shown below> Enter a valid email-id> Click Next.

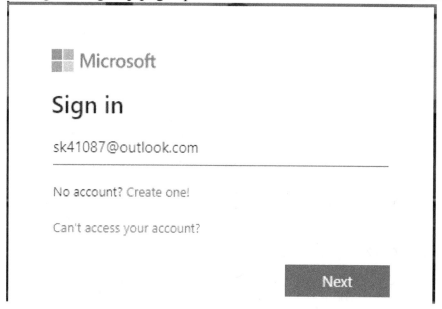

3. Enter Password of your email-id Account> Click Sign in.

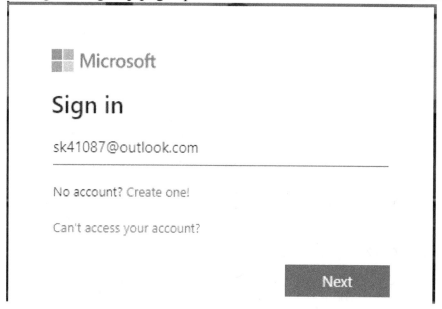

4. Azure Sign-up page opens as shown below> Your Name and email-id will be
   pre-populated> Enter your Mobile Number without any country code> Click Text me.

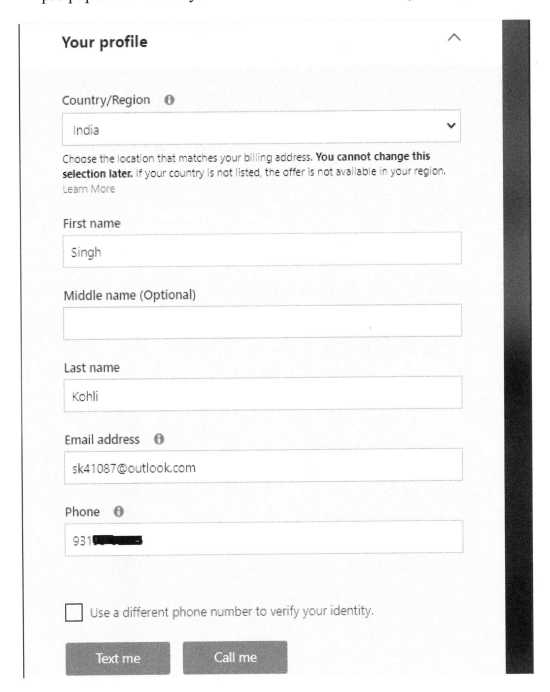

5. A verification code box will pop up below Text me Box> Enter the code received on your mobile number> Click Verify code.

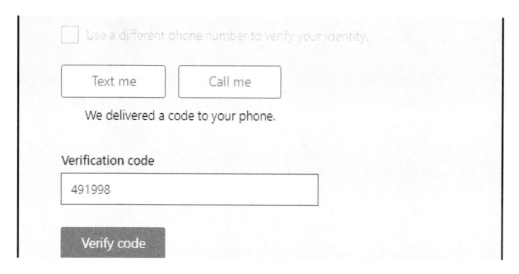

6. You will be still in Step 4 Figure> Enter Organization name. Enter any name here> Leave PAN ID blank. This will be specific for each Country from where you are signing. In my case I am signing from India. System is asking for PAN Card id> Select the check box for I agree option> Click Next.

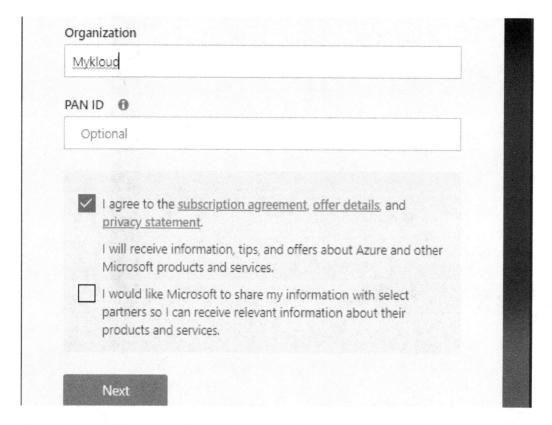

Note: Depending upon from where you sign-in, there is a possibility that you might not be asked for Organization name and/or PAN ID.

7. Identity verification by Card pane comes up as shown below> Enter Card details> Enter Address details> Click Sign up.

8. Process of setting up Azure Trial Account will start. Your credit card may charge a nominal amount> A signup feedback page might come up. Click Submit here.

9. You will be logged on to Quickstart Center of Azure Portal as shown below> I also clicked on the Notification icon. It is showing balance of Rupees 14500 (Equals to US Dollar 200).

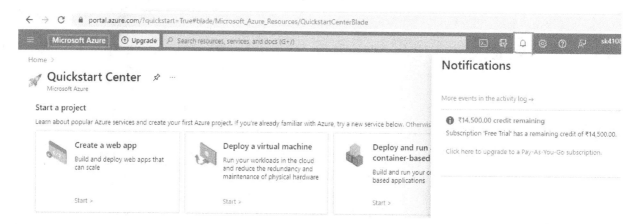

10. In above figure click Microsoft Azure> Azure Portal Home page opens as shown below.

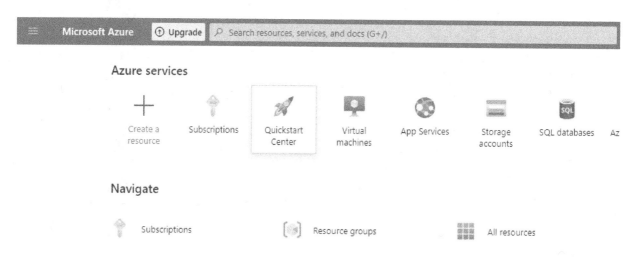

11. Readers are requested to Click Subscriptions in above figure to see details of their Subscription.

Disable Security Defaults in Azure AD

Security Default forces Azure AD Users to register for Multi-Factor Authentication (MFA) and automatically enables MFA for Administrators.

In next exercise we will disable Security Defaults in Azure AD. We are disabling Security Defaults because MFA using Security defaults does not provide all the features. In Chapter 8 we will enable MFA using Azure AD Premium P2 License.

Exercise 3.2: Disable Security Defaults

1. Open **Chrome Browser** and go to Azure Portal @ portal.azure.com> Azure Portal opens as shown below> Note the 3 Horizontal lines in top left.

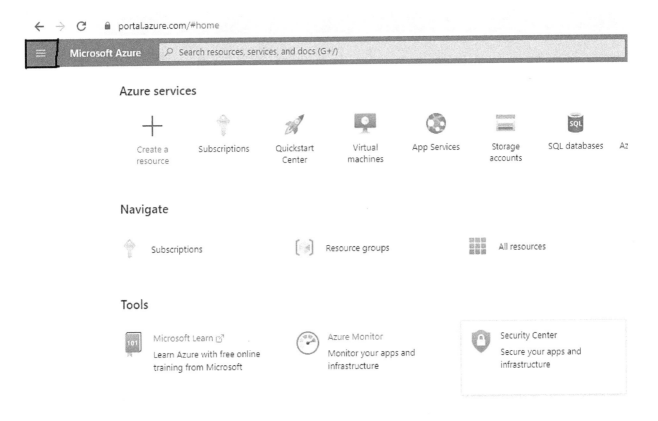

2. In above figure Click 3 Horizontal lines in top left> A dropdown pane opens in left of Azure Portal> Note the Azure Active Directory option in dropdown left pane.

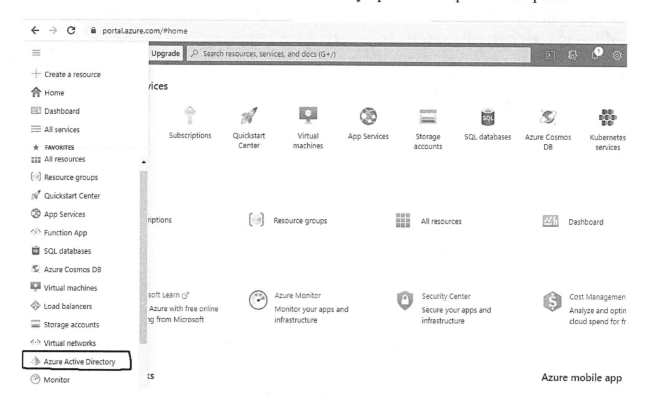

3. In above figure click Azure Active Directory in left pane> Azure AD Dashboard opens as shown below> Scroll down in left pane> Note the Properties option in left pane.

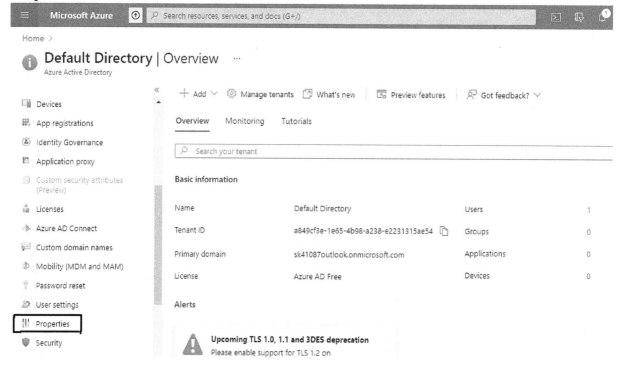

4. In above figure click Properties in left pane> Azure AD Tenant Properties blade opens in right pane as shown below> In right pane scroll down and note the **Manage Security defaults** link option.

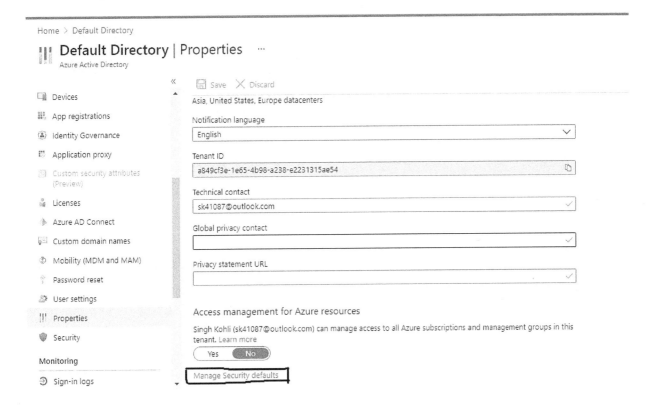

5. In above figure click **Manage Security defaults** link> Enable Security defaults pane opens as shown below> In Enable Security defaults Click **No**> Select a Reason and click Save.

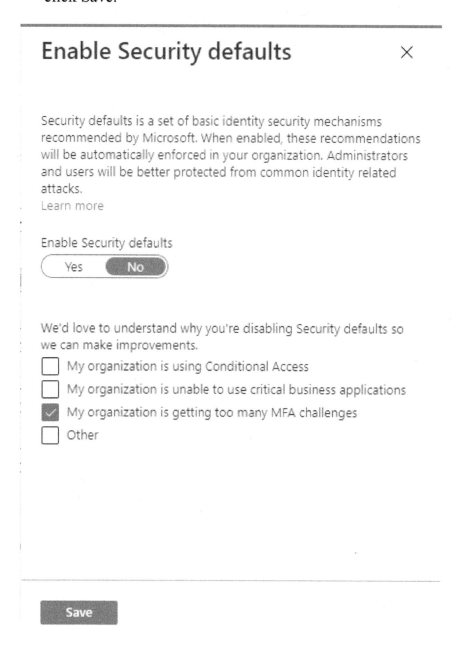

6. Close the Tenant Properties Pane.

Lab Requirements & Tricks

Resource Naming

In Exercises I keep referring to resources created in previous exercises. My suggestion would be that you name your resources by adding some letter or number to my resource names. The above suggestion is just for lab exercises in this book and not for your production use case.

Browser Requirements for Lab Exercises

You will require 2 Browsers for completing Lab Activities. I used following Browser options for completing lab activities.

1. **Chrome Browser** was my main Browser. I used it with Subscription User. This was the user with which I signed for Azure Subscription.
2. **Firefox Browser** was used with users created in Azure AD.

Important points regarding Lab Exercises

I used email address of sk41087@outlook.com and name Singh Kohli to create Azure Account.

This User has access to all **Azure Resources** and **Azure AD Resources.** We are calling this user as Subscription Administrator.

The Azure AD Username of this User is Singh Kohli.

Login name of Singh Kohli to Azure Portal is sk41087@outlook.com.

Most of the Administrative activity in this book will be performed by this User.

In your (Book Readers) case, Subscription Administrator Name will be the name which you have used to create Azure Account.

In your (Book Readers) case, Subscription Administrator's Login name for Azure Portal will be the email Account which you have used to create Azure Account.

1. All Exercises must be done using Chrome Browser and Subscription Administrator Credentials unless specified. This is the user with which you have signed for Azure Subscription. <u>For Exercises using Subscription Administrator I might not specify that I am using this option.</u>

2. When I am not mentioning anything while doing labs, it will mean that you have to login to Azure Portal using Subscription Administrator credentials in Chrome Browser.

3. For Users (User1, User2 etc) created in Azure AD I will mention them specifically when logging to Azure Portal. For Users created in Azure AD we will use Firefox Browser to login to Azure Portal.

Chapter 4 Azure Resource Groups

Introduction to Resource Groups

Resource Groups are logical containers in which resources are grouped. All Resources in Azure are created in Resource Group.

Resource groups allow you to manage related resources as a single unit. Using Resources Groups you can monitor, control access and manage billing for resources that are required to run an application.

Resource Group can be created independently or can be created along with resource creation.

Design Considerations for Resource Groups

1. A Resource Group can contain resources that reside in different regions.
2. All the resources in a resource group must be associated with a single subscription.
3. Each resource can only exist in one resource group.
4. You can move a resource from one Resource Group to another Resource Group.
5. Ideally all the resources in a resource group should share the same lifecycle. You deploy, update, and delete them together. If one resource, such as a database server, needs to exist on a different deployment cycle it should be in another resource group.
6. A Resource Group can be used to scope access control for administrative actions.

Exercise 4.1: Create Resource Group RGCloud

1. Open Chrome Browser and go to Azure Portal @ portal.azure.com> Azure Portal opens as shown below> Note the 3 Horizontal lines in top left.

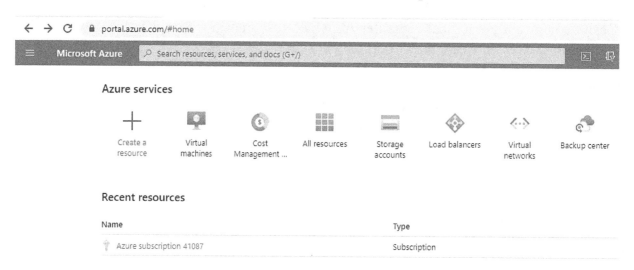

2. In above figure Click 3 Horizontal lines in top left> A pane opens in left of Azure Portal> Note the Resource groups option in dropdown left pane.

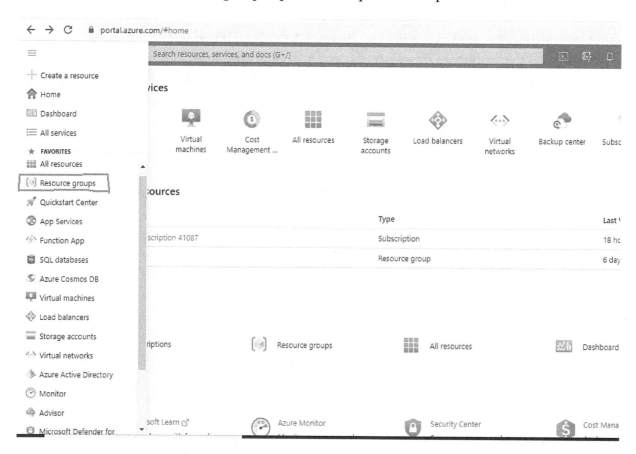

3. In above figure click Resource groups in left pane> All Resource Group pane opens. Click + Create> Create a Resource group blade opens as shown below> Enter a name. I entered RGCloud> In Region select **East US 2**> Click Review + create> After Validation is passed Click Create (Not Shown).

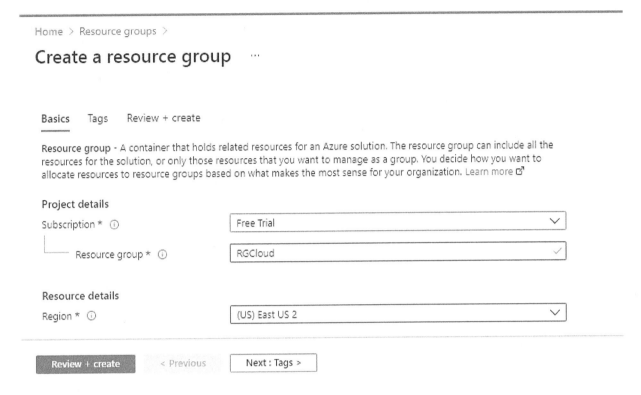

4. Figure below shows Resource Group RGCloud Dashboard. Currently there are no resources to display as it is a newly created group.

Chapter 5 Azure Virtual Network (VNET)

Azure Virtual Network (VNET)

An Azure Virtual Network (VNET) is Virtual Data Centre in the cloud. Virtual Network is further segmented into subnets. Virtual Machines are created in Subnets.

Virtual Network Subnets

VNET is divided into subnets. Subnets are assigned IP addresses by Subnetting VNET network address space. Access to the subnet can be controlled through Network Security groups (NSG). User defined route (UDR) tables can also be assigned to subnets. Virtual Machines are created in Subnets.

Figure below shows Virtual Network KNET with 2 Subnets – Web-Subnet and DB-Subnet. There are 3 virtual machines in these subnets.

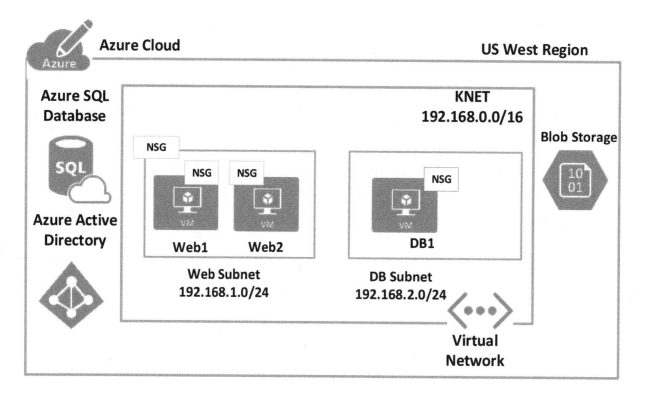

Virtual Network is created by the customer. Resources within Virtual Network are created and managed by end customers. Whereas Resources outside of VNET (Azure SQL, Azure AD etc) are Azure Managed Resources with Public IPs. Azure Managed Resources are not only accessed by VMs in VNET but are also accessed through internet.

Default Communication within and between Subnets

1. All VM to VM traffic within subnet or between subnets is allowed.
2. VM to internet traffic is allowed.
3. Azure Load balancer to VM is allowed.
4. Inbound internet to VM is blocked.

Note: Default rules can be overridden by new rules you create using NSG.

Private Address Range for Virtual Networks

You can use following class A, Class B and Class C address range for virtual networks.

10.0.0.0/8
172.16.0.0/12
192.168.0.0/16

Once the IP address range is decided, we can then divide this range into subnets. Virtual Machines NICs in the subnet are assigned private IP addresses via Azure DHCP from the subnet network address range.

Exercise 5.1: Create Virtual Network VNETCloud and Subnet Web-Subnet

In this Exercise we will create Virtual Network with name VNETCloud. Virtual Network VNETCloud will be created in Resource Group RGCloud and in Region East US 2. Resource Group RGCloud was created in Exercise 4.1 in Chapter 4.

1. Open Chrome Browser and go to Azure Portal @ portal.azure.com> Azure Portal opens. In Azure Portal Click 3 Horizontal lines in top left> A pane opens in left of Azure Portal as shown below> Note the Virtual networks option in left pane.

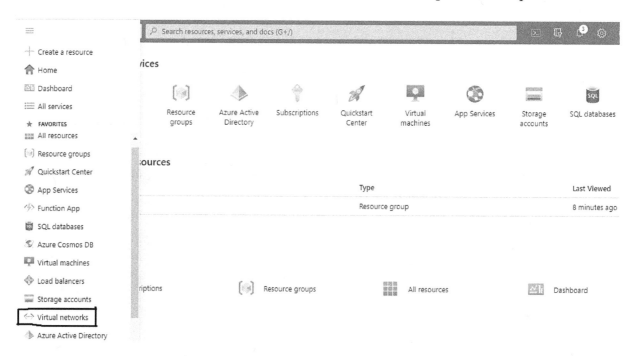

2. In above figure click Virtual networks> All Virtual networks pane opens as shown below> Note the + Create option.

3. In above figure click + Create> Create virtual network blade opens as shown below>
   In Resource Group select RGCloud> In name I entered VNETCloud> In Region
   select East US 2> Click Next: IP Adresses.

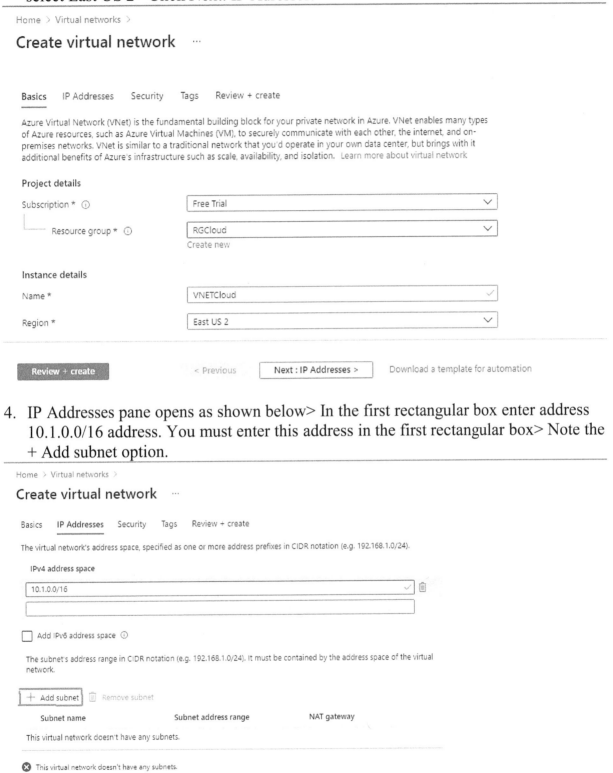

4. IP Addresses pane opens as shown below> In the first rectangular box enter address
   10.1.0.0/16 address. You must enter this address in the first rectangular box> Note the
   + Add subnet option.

5. In above figure Click + Add subnet > Add subnet blade opens in extreme right as shown below> In name enter **Web-Subnet**>In Subnet address range enter **10.1.1.0/24**> Rest select all default values>Click Add> You will be back in IP Addresses blade> Click Review + create> After Validation is passed click Create (Not Shown).

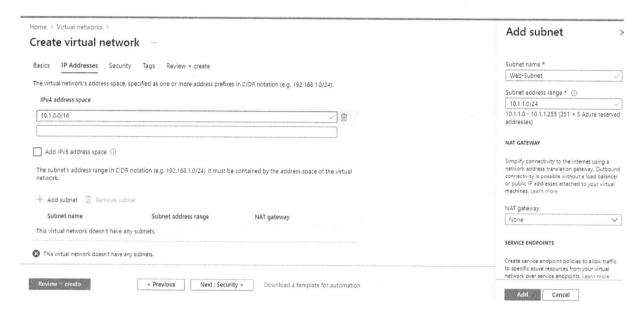

6. Figure below shows the dashboard of Virtual Network VNETCloud.

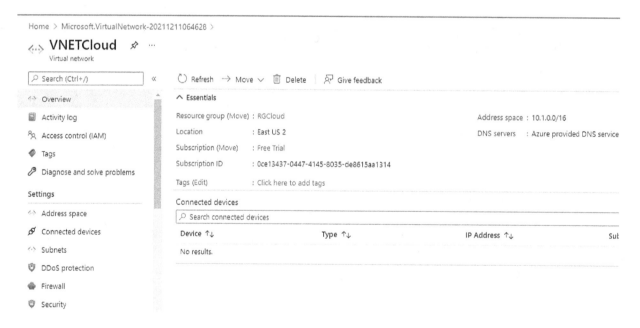

Chapter 6 Azure Compute

Azure Virtual Machine is on-demand resizable computing resource in the cloud that can be used to host variety of applications. Azure Virtual Machine runs on a Hyper-V host which also runs other Virtual Machines.

You can scale up by using bigger size Virtual Machine or scale out using additional instance of the virtual machine and then Load Balancing them.
Azure VM can be Windows or Linux based.

Virtual Machines Series

Virtual Machines series in Azure can be categorized under General purpose, Compute optimized, Memory optimized, Storage Optimized, GPU and High Performance Compute.

Type	Series	Description
General purpose	Bs, Av2, D2as, D2ads, D2a, D2as, D2d, D2 & D2s	Balanced CPU-to-memory ratio. Ideal for testing and development, General Purpose Production workloads, small to medium databases, and low to medium traffic web servers.
Compute optimized	FSv2, F, Fs & FX	High CPU-to-memory ratio. Good for medium traffic web servers, network appliances, batch processes, and application servers.
Memory optimized	E2, E2s, E2bds, E2bs, E2d, E2ds, EC, Dv2, G, M, & Mv2	High memory-to-core ratio. Great for relational database servers, medium to large caches, and in-memory analytics.
Storage optimized	Lsv2, Ls	High disk throughput and IO. Ideal for Big Data, SQL, and NoSQL databases.
GPU	NC, NCs, NV, NDs & ND	Specialized virtual machines targeted for heavy graphic rendering and video editing. Available with single or multiple GPUs.
High performance compute	H, Hb, HBv2, HBv3 & Hc	High Performance Computing VMs are good for high performance & parallel computing workloads such as financial risk modeling, seismic and reservoir simulation, molecular modeling and genomic research.

Note: Microsoft recommends that to get the best performance for price, use the latest generation VMs.

Virtual Machine Disk Types

Storage for Virtual Machines is provided by Virtual Machine Disks. Azure Virtual Machine Disks (OS & Data) are stored in Page Blobs.

Azure Virtual Machine Disks can use Standard Storage or Premium Storage. Standard Storage is backed by Magnetic HDD and Premium Storage is backed by SSD.

Azure Virtual Machines have minimum of 2 disks: **OS Disk (Labelled as C drive)** and **Temporary Disk (Labelled as D drive).** You can also attach additional **Data Disks.**

Virtual Machine Disks (OS and Data disk) are accessed over the network. Temporary disk is located on the physical host where the virtual machine is running a shown below.

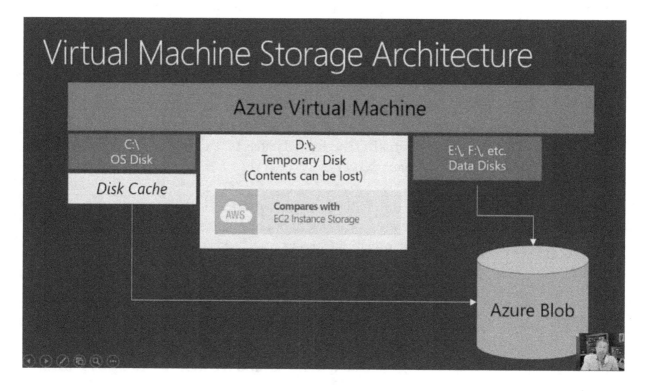

Azure Virtual Machine disk types (OS & Data Disk) can be Unmanaged or Managed. MS recommends that Managed Disk option to be used for all new VMs. This Chapter will focus on Managed Disks only.

Virtual Machine High Availability

To provide Virtual Machine High Availability you require following:

- Minimum 2 Instances of Virtual Machines which are Load Balanced using Load Balancers.
- Underlying Infrastructure high availability using either **Availability Set (AS)** or **Availability Zones (AZ).** Availability Set (AS) or Availability Zones (AZ) options are chosen during VM creation time as shown below.

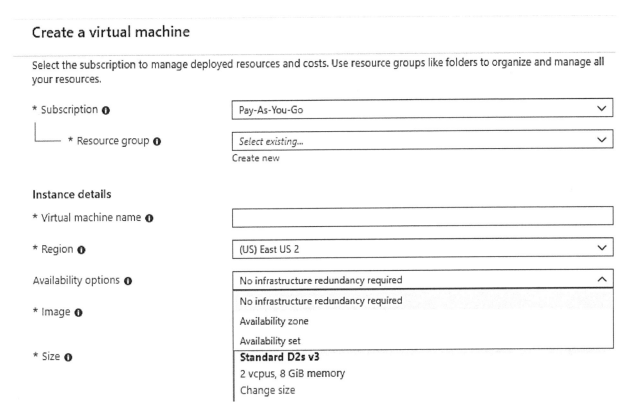

Important Note 1: Detailed discussion on Availability Set (AS) and Availability Zones (AZ) is beyond the scope of this Book.

Important Note 2: In upcoming Exercises we will be not using Availability Set (AS) or Availability Zones (AZ) options while creating Virtual Machines. Instead we will use option No Infrastructure Redundancy required.

VM High Availability using Availability Set (AS)

Availability Set (AS) Provides high Availability against hardware failure in Azure Cloud by eliminating single point of failure.

By creating an **Availability Set** and adding virtual machines to the Availability Set, Azure will ensure that the virtual machines in the set get distributed across the physical hosts, Network switch & Rack that run them in such a way that a hardware failure will not bring down all the machines in the set.
Each virtual machine in the Availability Set is assigned an update domain and a fault domain by Azure.

An **Update Domain (UD)** is used to determine the sets of virtual machines and the underlying hardware that can be rebooted together. For each Availability Set created, five Update Domains will be created by default, but can be changed. You can configure Maximum of 20 Update Domains. When Microsoft is updating physical host it will reboot only one update domain at a time.

Fault domains (FD) define the group of virtual machines that share a common power source and network switch. For each Availability Set, two Fault Domains will be created by default, but can be changed. You can configure Maximum of 3 Fault Domains.

VM High Availability using Availability Zones (AZ)

Azure Availability Zone protects your applications and data from Complete Location breakdown or Datacenter wide outage which affects the entire Azure Data Center.

To Provide High Availability to VMs you need to create VMs in different Availability Zones and Load Balance them with a Load Balancer.

Figure below shows Azure Standard Load Balancer providing cross-zone Load Balancing to 3 VMs located in AZ1, AZ2 and AZ3 respectively.

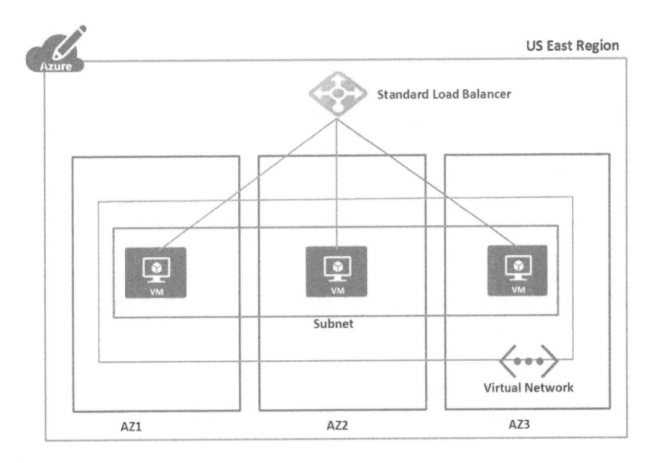

Exercise 6.1: Create Windows Virtual Machine vmcloud1

In this exercise we will create Windows Server 2019 VM vmcloud1 in Subnet Web-Subnet of Virtual Network **VNETCloud** (Created in Exercise 5.1 in Chapter 5) and in Resource Group **RGCloud** (Created in Exercise 4.1 in Chapter 4) and in East US 2 Region.

1. Open Chrome Browser and log on to Azure Portal @ portal.azure.com using Subscription Administrator credentials and password> Azure Portal opens as shown below. In Azure Portal Click 3 Horizontal lines in top left> A pane opens in left of Azure Portal as shown below> Note the Virtual machines option in left pane.

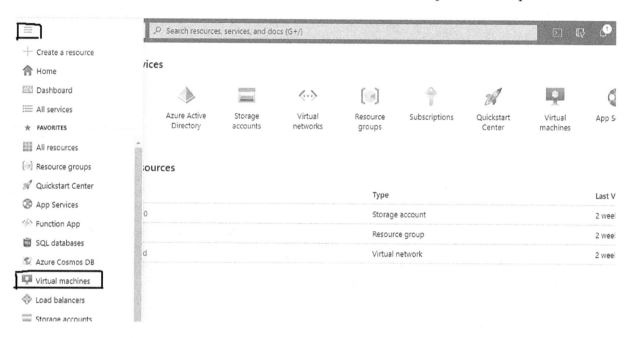

2. In above figure click Virtual machines> All Virtual machines pane opens as shown below> Note the + Create option.

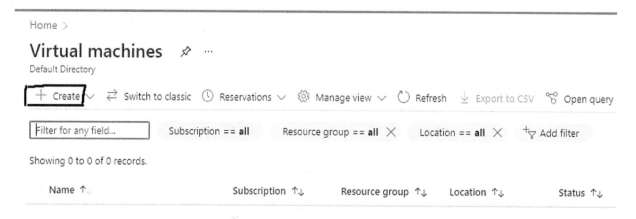

3. Click + Create in above figure and then Click + Virtual machine from dropdown pane> Create a virtual machine Blade opens as shown below> Select Resource Group RGCloud> Enter a name. I entered vmcloud1> In Region select East US 2> **In Availability options select No**> In Security type select Standard> In Image select Windows Server 2019 Datacenter-Gen2> For size select the default option> Enter Username. I entered AdminAccount> Enter Password and Confirm Password> select Allow selected ports for Public inbound ports and select Ports 80, 443 and 3389> Click Next: Disks (Not Shown).

Home > Virtual machines >

Create a virtual machine ···

Resource group * ⓘ	RGCloud ∨
	Create new

Instance details

Virtual machine name * ⓘ	vmcloud1
Region * ⓘ	(US) East US 2 ∨
Availability options ⓘ	No infrastructure redundancy required ∨
Security type ⓘ	Standard ∨
Image * ⓘ	⊞ Windows Server 2019 Datacenter - Gen2 ∨
	See all images	Configure VM generation
Azure Spot instance ⓘ	☐
Size * ⓘ	Standard_D2s_v3 - 2 vcpus, 8 GiB memory (₹9,887.49/month) ∨

Administrator account

Username * ⓘ	AdminAcount
Password * ⓘ	············
Confirm password * ⓘ	············

Inbound port rules

Select which virtual machine network ports are accessible from the public internet. You can specify more limited or granular network access on the Networking tab.

Public inbound ports * ⓘ	◯ None
	⦿ Allow selected ports
Select inbound ports *	HTTP (80), HTTPS (443), RDP (3389) ∨
	☑ HTTP (80)
	☑ HTTPS (443)
	☐ SSH (22)
	☑ RDP (3389)

4. Disk Screen opens>Select your OS disk Option. I selected Standard SSD> Rest Select all Default values>Click Next: Networking (Not Shown).

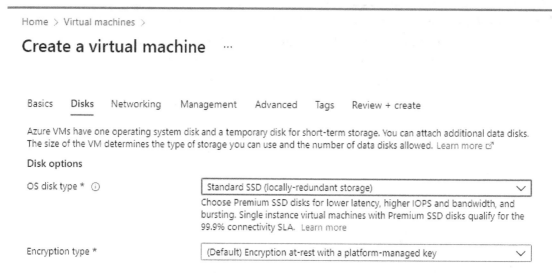

5. Networking pane opens as shown below> In Virtual Network Select **VNETCloud**> In Subnet Select **Web-Subnet** > In Public IP option keep system selected name. In Public IP click link Create new. Create public IP address blades opens in right. In name keep system selected name. In SKU select **Standard.** In Assignment select **Static**. Click Ok>Make sure that in NIC network security group **Basic** is selected>In Public inbound ports select **Allow Selected Ports** and make sure **HTTP (80), HTTPS (443)** and **RDP (3389) are selected** > Rest Select all default values> Click **Next: Management.**

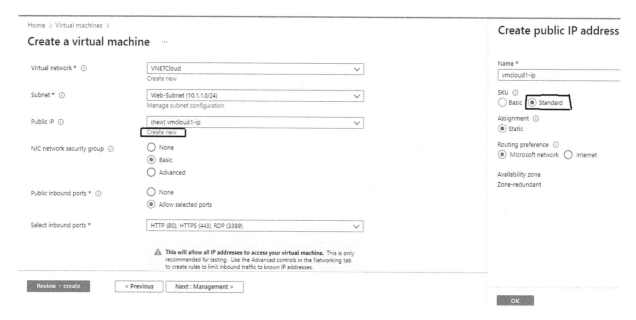

Note: Note the Network security group Basic option This will create Network security group which will be applied to Network Interface of VM vmcloud1.

6. Management Screen opens as shown below> In Azure Security Center deselect Enable basic plan for free> Rest select all default values> **Click Review + create.** We are selecting default values for Advanced and Tags options

---

Home > Virtual machines >

Create a virtual machine ...

Basics   Disks   Networking   **Management**   Advanced   Tags   Review + create

Configure monitoring and management options for your VM.

Azure Security Center

Azure Security Center provides unified security management and advanced threat protection across hybrid cloud workloads. Learn more ⟋

| Enable basic plan for free ⓘ | ☐ | |
| | | This will apply to every VM in the selected subscription |

Monitoring

Boot diagnostics ⓘ
- ⦿ Enable with managed storage account (recommended)
- ○ Enable with custom storage account
- ○ Disable

Enable OS guest diagnostics ⓘ   ☐

Identity

System assigned managed identity ⓘ   ☐

Azure AD

Login with Azure AD ⓘ   ☐

ⓘ RBAC role assignment of Virtual Machine Administrator Login or Virtual Machine User Login is required when using Azure AD login. Learn more ⟋

Auto-shutdown

Enable auto-shutdown ⓘ   ☐

Backup

Enable backup ⓘ   ☐

Site Recovery

Enable Disaster Recovery ⓘ   ☐

Guest OS updates

Enable hotpatch (Preview) ⓘ   ☐

Patch orchestration options ⓘ   [Automatic by OS (Windows Automatic Updates)   ⌄]

[Review + create]   [< Previous]   [Next : Advanced >]

7. After validation is passed, Review + create Screen opens as shown below>click Create.

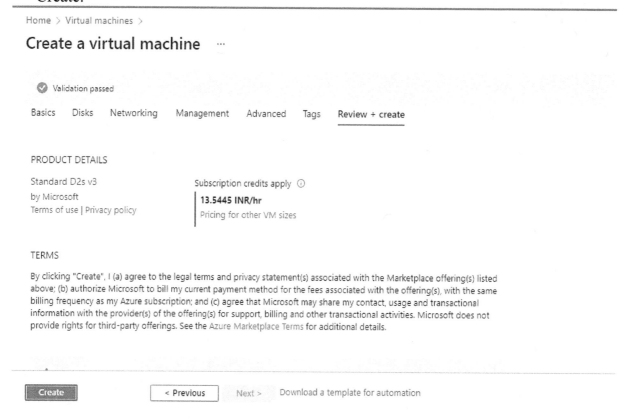

8. Deployment of VM vmcloud1 will begin. After deployment is finished click **Go to Resource**> Figure below shows the dashboard of Virtual Machine vmcloud1> Note the Not Configures option in right pane. We will use this option in next step to configure vmcloud1 DNS name. Also note the Connect option. We will use this option in next Exercise to Download RDP File.

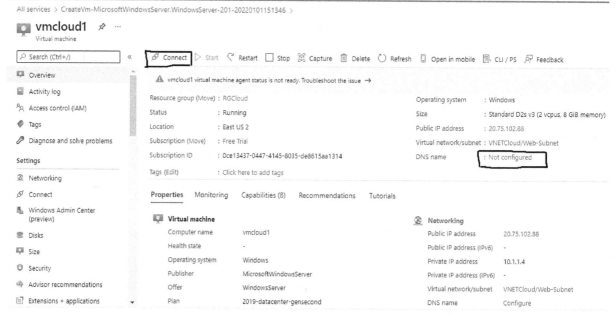

9. **In this step we will assign DNS name to VM vmcloud1.**
   In above figure Click Not Configured in right pane>Public IP Address pane opens as shown below> Under DNS name label enter DNS name for your VM. I entered **vmcloud1**> Click **Save**> After notification of success close the Pubic IP pane.
   Note: In Book readers case they need to enter a different DNS name.

10. Back in VM vmcloud1 dashboard Click Refresh one or two times and you can see the DNS name of vmcloud1 (vmcloud1.eastus2.cloudapp.azure.com) in DNS name row> Note the Connect option. I clicked it and a dropdown pane opens. Note the RDP option> We will use this option to download RDP file based on DNS address in next exercise.

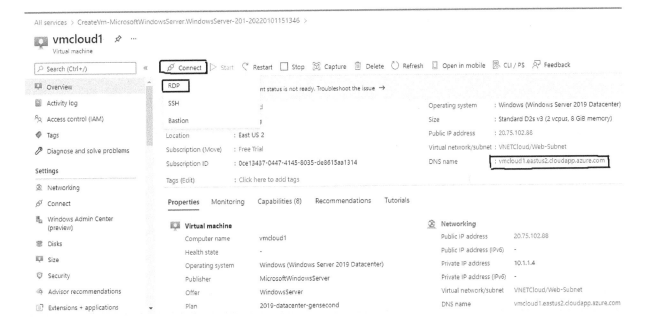

Exercise 6.2: Log on to Windows VM vmcloud1 with RDP

1. Go to VM vmcloud1 dashboard and click **Connect** in right pane> A dropdown box opens. Note the RDP option> Click RDP>Connect with RDP pane opens as shown below> Make sure DNS name is selected in IP Address Box> Click **download RDP file** to download RDP file on your desktop. Close the Connect option pane.

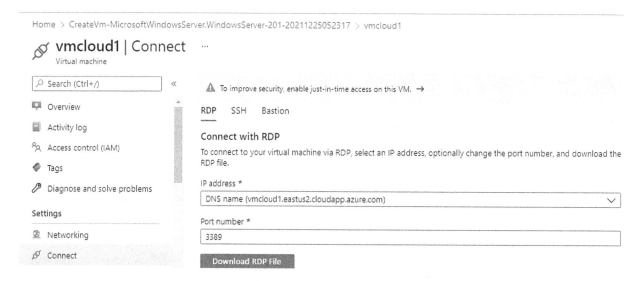

2. On your desktop Click the downloaded RDP file>Click Connect>Credential box for connecting to VM will Pop up on your desktop. Enter the Administrator Account Username and password you entered during VM creation (Step 3 in Exercise 6.1) and click OK.

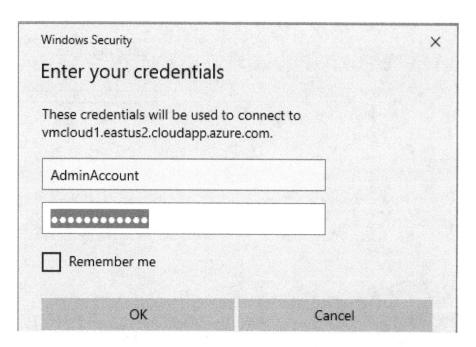

3. Figure below shows the screen of Windows VM vmfe1 with Server Manager open. Note the **Add roles and feature** option in right pane. In exercise 4 we will use this option to Install IIS.

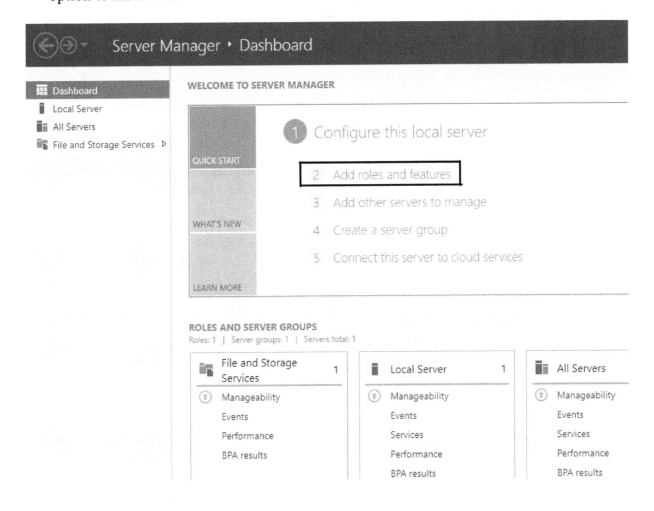

4. Keep the RDP pane open. We need to use it in next Exercise.

Exercise 6.3: Install IIS on VM vmcloud1

1. In Server Manager Dashboard Click **Add roles and features** link as shown in previous page figure>Add Roles and Feature Wizard opens as shown below> Click Next.

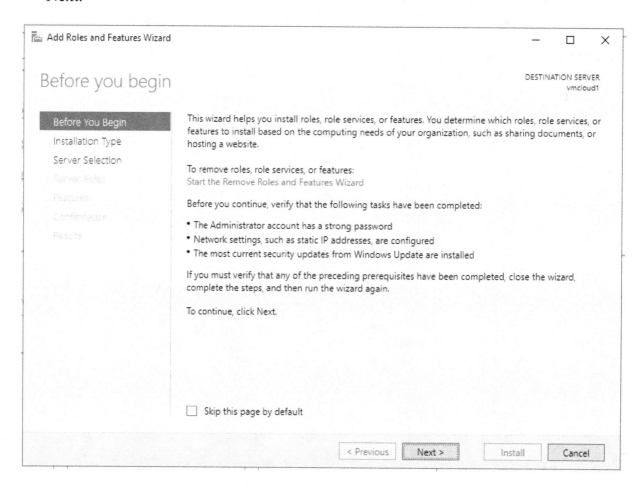

2. Select Installation Type pane opens> Choose **Role-based or feature-based installation**, and then click Next.
3. Select Destination Server pane opens> Make sure that Select a server from server pool option is selected> Select VM vmcloud1 and click Next.

4. Select Server Roles pane opens as shown below> select **Web Server (IIS)**> A Box about adding features that are required for IIS pops up> Make sure that Include management tools is selected> Click Add Features> You will be back in Select Server Roles pane> click Next in the wizard.

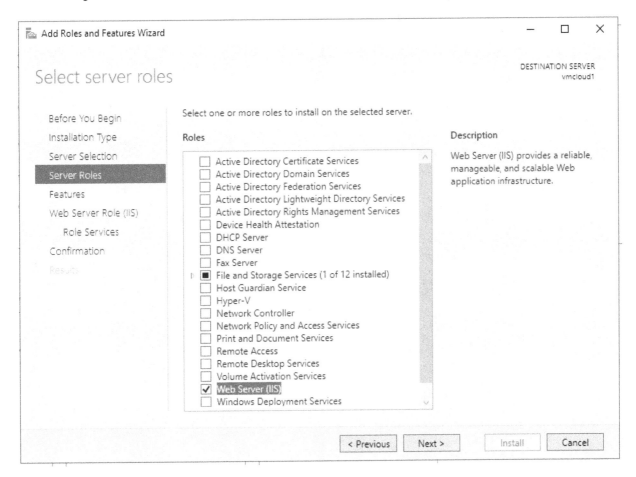

5. Click next, next, next.
6. Click Install. It will take around 1 – 2 minutes to install the IIS. After Installation is complete click close> Close RDP Pane also.

Exercise 6.4: Access Default IIS website on VM vmcloud1

1. Go to VM vmcloud1 dashboard and note down DNS name> In my case it was **vmcloud1.eastus2.cloudapp.azure.com.**
2. Open chrome browser tab on your desktop/laptop and type: **vmcloud1.eastus2.cloudapp.azure.com.**
3. The default website on VM vmcloud1 opens as shown below.

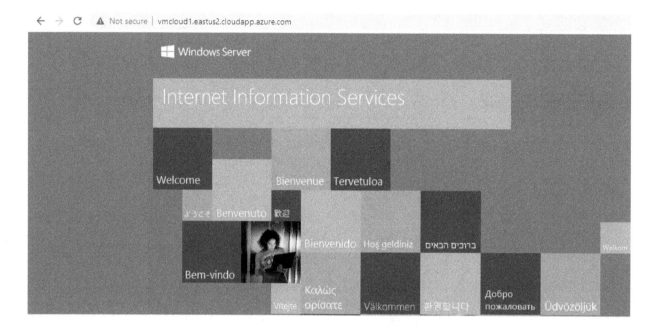

Exercise 6.5: Create Windows Virtual Machine vmcloud2

In this exercise we will create Windows Server 2019 VM with name vmcloud2 in Subnet Web-Subnet of Virtual Network **VNETCloud** (Created in Exercise 5.1 in Chapter 5) and in Resource Group **RGCloud** (Created in Exercise 4.1 in Chapter 4) and in East US 2 Region.

1. Open Chrome Browser and log on to Azure Portal @ portal.azure.com using Subscription Administrator credentials and password> Azure Portal opens as shown below. In Azure Portal Click 3 Horizontal lines in top left> A pane opens in left of Azure Portal as shown below> Note the Virtual machines option in left pane.

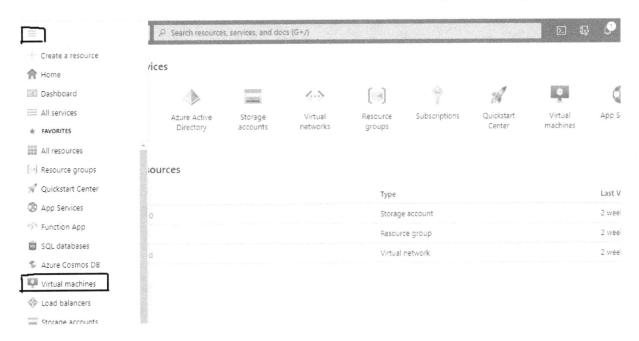

2. In above figure click Virtual machines> All Virtual machines pane opens as shown below> Note the + Create option.

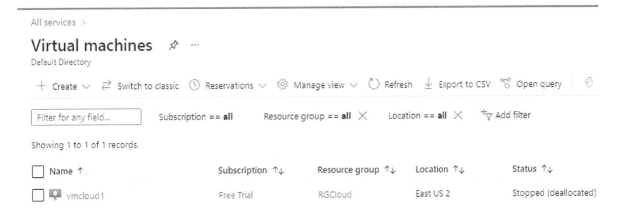

3. Click + Create in above figure and then Click + Virtual machine from dropdown pane> Create virtual machine Blade opens as shown below> Select Resource Group RGCloud> Enter a name. I entered vmcloud2> In Region select East US 2> **In Availability options select No**> In Security type select Standard> In Image select Windows Server 2019 Datacenter-Gen2> For size select the default option> Enter Username. I entered AdminAccount> Enter Password and Confirm Password> select Allow selected ports for Public inbound ports and select Ports 80, 443 and 3389> Click Next: Disks (Not Shown).

Home >

Create a virtual machine   ...

Resource group * ⓘ	RGCloud ▼
	Create new

Instance details

Virtual machine name * ⓘ	vmcloud2 ✓
Region * ⓘ	(US) East US 2 ▼
Availability options ⓘ	No infrastructure redundancy required ▼
Security type ⓘ	Standard ▼
Image * ⓘ	⊞ Windows Server 2019 Datacenter - Gen2 ▼
	See all images | Configure VM generation
Azure Spot instance ⓘ	☐
Size * ⓘ	Standard_D2s_v3 - 2 vcpus, 8 GiB memory (₹9,887.49/month) ▼
	See all sizes

Administrator account

Username * ⓘ	AdminAcount ✓
Password * ⓘ	••••••••••• ✓
Confirm password * ⓘ	••••••••••• ✓

Inbound port rules

Select which virtual machine network ports are accessible from the public internet. You can specify more limited or granular network access on the Networking tab.

Public inbound ports * ⓘ	○ None
	◉ Allow selected ports
Select inbound ports *	HTTP (80), HTTPS (443), RDP (3389) ▼
	☑ HTTP (80)
	☑ HTTPS (443)
	☐ SSH (22)
	☑ RDP (3389)

4. Disk Screen opens>Select your OS disk Option. I selected Standard SSD> Rest Select all Default values>Click Next: Networking (Not Shown).

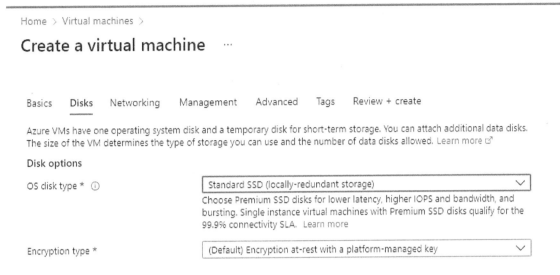

5. Networking pane opens as shown below> In Virtual Network Select **VNETCloud**> In Subnet Select **Web-Subnet** > In Public IP option keep system selected name. In Public IP click link Create new. Create public IP address blades opens in right. In name keep system selected name. In SKU select **Standard.** In Assignment select **Static.** Click Ok>Make sure that in NIC network security group **Basic** is selected>In Public inbound ports select **Allow Selected Ports** and make sure **HTTP (80), HTTPS (443) and RDP (3389) are selected** > Rest Select all default values> Click **Review + create**> Please note that we are selecting default values for Management, Advanced and Tag options.

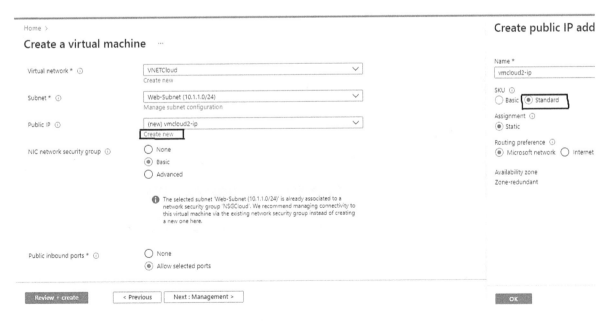

Note: Note the Network security group Basic option This will create Network security group which will be applied to Network Interface of VM vmcloud1.

6. Management Screen opens as shown below> In Azure Security Center deselect Enable basic plan for free> Rest select all default values> **Click Review + create.** We are selecting default values for Advanced and Tags options

Home > Virtual machines >

Create a virtual machine ···

Basics   Disks   Networking   **Management**   Advanced   Tags   Review + create

Configure monitoring and management options for your VM.

Azure Security Center

Azure Security Center provides unified security management and advanced threat protection across hybrid cloud workloads. Learn more ↗

Enable basic plan for free ⓘ   ☐

This will apply to every VM in the selected subscription

Monitoring

Boot diagnostics ⓘ   ◉ Enable with managed storage account (recommended)
⭕ Enable with custom storage account
⭕ Disable

Enable OS guest diagnostics ⓘ   ☐
Identity

System assigned managed identity ⓘ   ☐

Azure AD

Login with Azure AD ⓘ   ☐

ⓘ RBAC role assignment of Virtual Machine Administrator Login or Virtual Machine User Login is required when using Azure AD login. Learn more ↗

Auto-shutdown

Enable auto-shutdown ⓘ   ☐

Backup

Enable backup ⓘ   ☐

Site Recovery

Enable Disaster Recovery ⓘ   ☐
Guest OS updates

Enable hotpatch (Preview) ⓘ   ☐

Patch orchestration options ⓘ   [Automatic by OS (Windows Automatic Updates)   ⌄]

[Review + create]   [< Previous]   [Next : Advanced >]

7. Review + create Screen opens as shown below> Click Create.

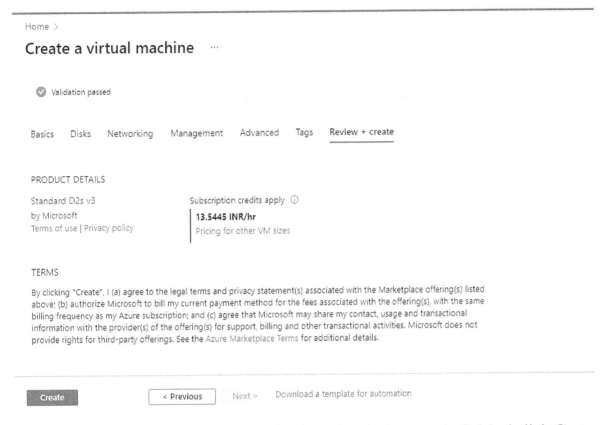

8. Deployment of VM vmcloud2 will begin. After deployment is finished click **Go to Resource**> Figure below shows the dashboard of Virtual Machine vmcloud2> Note the Not configured option in right pane. We will use this option in next step to configure vmcloud1 DNS name.

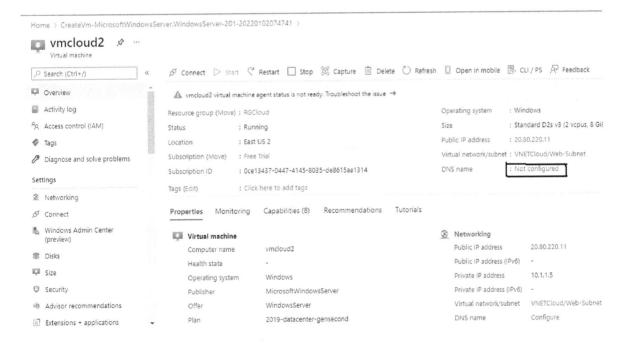

9. **In this step we will assign DNS name to VM vmcloud2.**
   In above figure Click Not configured in right pane>Public IP Address pane opens as shown below> Under DNS name label enter DNS name for your VM. I entered **vmcloud2**> Click **Save**> After notification of success close the Pubic IP pane.
   Note: In Book readers case they need to enter a different DNS name.

10. Back in VM vmcloud2 dashboard Click Refresh one or two times and you can see the DNS name of VM vmcloud2 (vmcloud2.eastus2.cloudapp.azure.com) in DNS name row> Note the Connect option. I clicked it and a dropdown pane opens. Note the RDP option> We will use this option to download RDP file based on DNS address in next exercise.

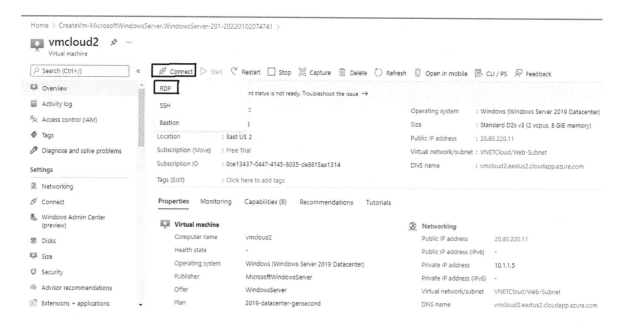

Exercise 6.6: Log on to Windows VM vmcloud2 with RDP

1. Go to VM vmcloud2 dashboard and click **Connect** in right pane> A dropdown box opens. Note the RDP option> Click RDP>Connect with RDP pane opens as shown below> Make sure DNS name is selected in IP Address Box> Click **download RDP file** to download RDP file on your desktop. Close the Connect option pane.

2. On your desktop Click the downloaded RDP file>Click Connect>Credential box for connecting to VM will Pop up on your desktop. Enter the Administrator Account Username and password you entered during VM creation (Step 3 in Exercise 6.5) and click OK.

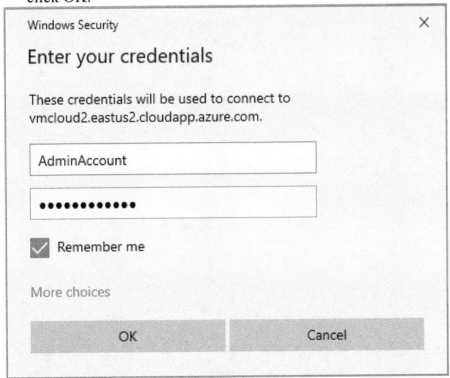

3. Figure below shows the screen of Windows VM vmcloud2 with Server Manager open. Note the **Add roles and feature** option in right pane. In exercise 4 we will use this option to Install IIS.

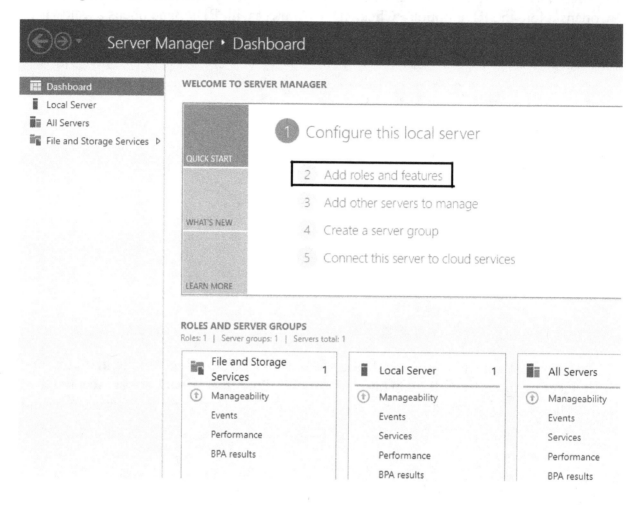

4. Keep the RDP pane open. We need to use it in next Exercise.

Exercise 6.7: Install IIS on VM vmcloud2

1. In server Manager Dashboard Click **Add roles and features** link as shown in previous page figure>Add Roles and Feature Wizard opens as shown below> Click Next.

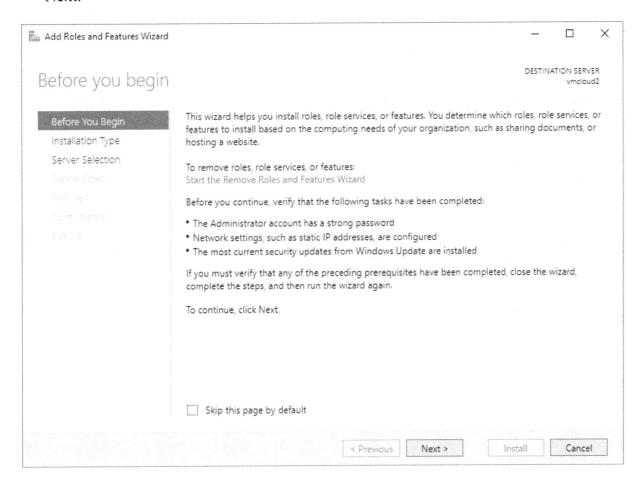

2. Select Installation Type pane opens> Choose **Role-based or feature-based installation**, and then click Next.
3. Select Destination Server pane opens> Make sure that Select a server from server pool option is selected> Select VM vmcloud2 and click Next.

4. Select Server Roles pane opens as shown below> select **Web Server (IIS)**> A Box about adding features that are required for IIS pops up> Make sure that Include management tools is selected> Click Add Features> You will be back in Select Server Roles pane> click Next in the wizard.

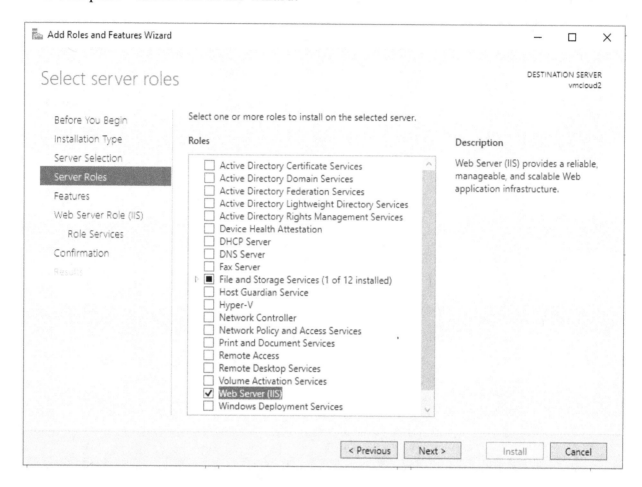

5. Click next, next, next.
6. Click Install. It will take around 1 – 2 minutes to install the IIS. After Installation is complete click close> Keep the RDP pane open. We require it in next Exercise.

Exercise 6.8: Create Custom Website on VM vmcloud2

1. You are already Logged on VM vmcloud2 through RDP>Minimize Server Manager> In VM vmcloud2 RDP pane right click on Desktop> Click New>Click Text Document> Notepad opens> Enter following in the Notepad.

```
<!DOCTYPE html>
<html>
<head>
<title>Azure Guide</title>
<meta charset="utf-8">
</head>
<body>
<h1>Azure Study & Lab Guide for Beginners</h1>
<p> Author: Harinder Kohli </p>
</body>
</html>
```

2. **Save the file as index.html. <u>Save the file in C:\inetpub\wwwroot folder</u>>** Close the Notepad.

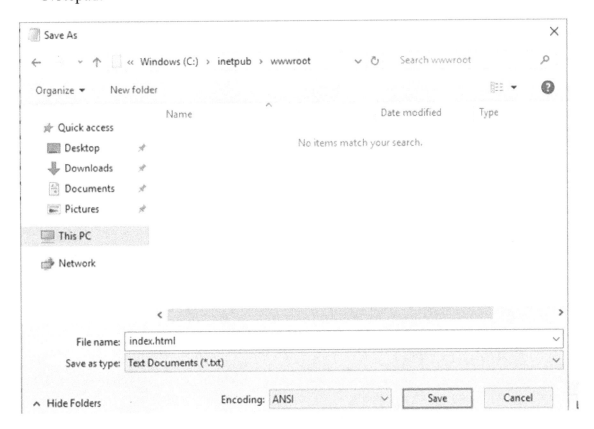

Exercise 6.9: Access Custom IIS website on VM vmcloud2

1. Go to VM vmcloud2 dashboard and note down DNS name> In my case it was **vmcloud2.eastus2.cloudapp.azure.com.**
2. Open chrome browser tab on your desktop/laptop and type: **vmcloud2.eastus2.cloudapp.azure.com.**
3. Custom website on VM vmcloud2 opens as shown below.

← → C ⚠ Not secure | vmcloud2.eastus2.cloudapp.azure.com

Azure Study & Lab Guide for Beginners

Author: Harinder Kohli

Exercise 6.10: Add Data Disk to VM vmcloud2 (Created in Exercise 6.5)

1. Go to VM vmcloud2 dashboard> Click Disks in left pane> In right pane note the + Create and attach a new disk option.

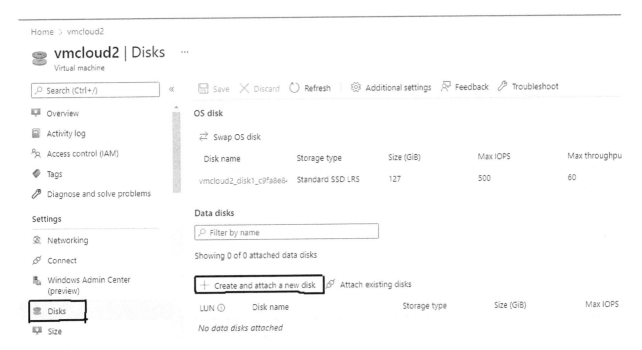

2. In above figure Click + Create and attach a new disk > Add disk pane opens under Data disks>In LUN dropdown box Select 2> Enter name for Data Disk> In Storage type box I selected Standard SSD> Rest Select all default values> Click Save.

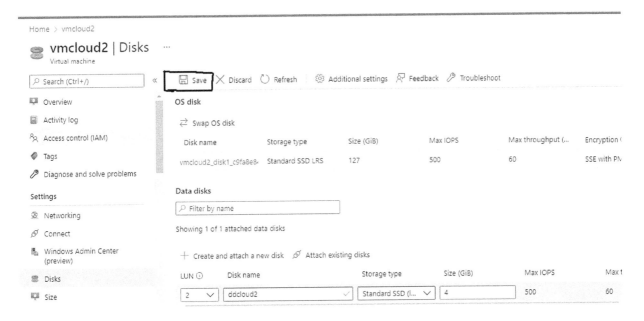

3. In VM vmcloud2 Disk pane you can now see that Data Disk ddcloud2 is added.

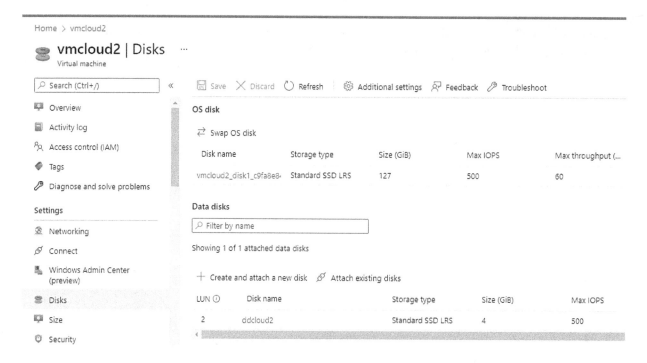

Exercise 6.11: Initialize the Data Disk

1. RDP to Virtual Machine vmcloud2. The procedure to RDP to Virtual Machine was shown in Exercise 6.6.
2. Open Server Manager> In the left pane note the File and Storage Services option.

3. In above figure click File and Storage Services in left pane> Note the Disks option in File and Storage Services pane.

4. In above figure Click Disks> The Disks section lists the disks. The Disk 0 is the operating system Disk. Disk 1 is the temporary disk. Disk 2 is the Data Disk. The Data disk you just added will list the Partition as Unknown> Select Data Disk with Number 2.

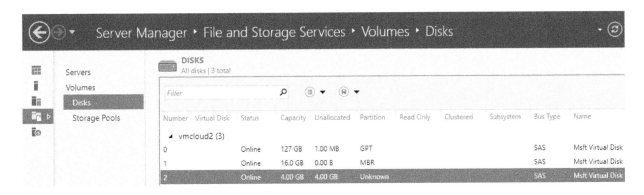

5. Right-click the Disk with number 2 and select Initialize> Click Yes. The Partition will now be listed as GPT.

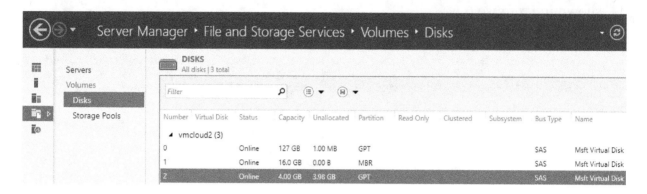

Chapter 7 Azure Storage

Introduction to Azure Storage

Azure Storage is a massively scalable object store for data objects, disk storage for Azure virtual machines (VMs), a file system service for the cloud, a messaging store for reliable messaging, and a NoSQL store.

Azure Storage Provides following 5 Data Storage Services:

Azure Blobs: A massively scalable object store for text and binary data.
Azure Files: Managed file shares for cloud or on-premises deployments.
Azure Queues: A messaging store for reliable messaging between application components.
Azure Tables: A NoSQL store for schemaless storage of structured data.
Azure Disks: Block-level storage volumes for Azure VMs.

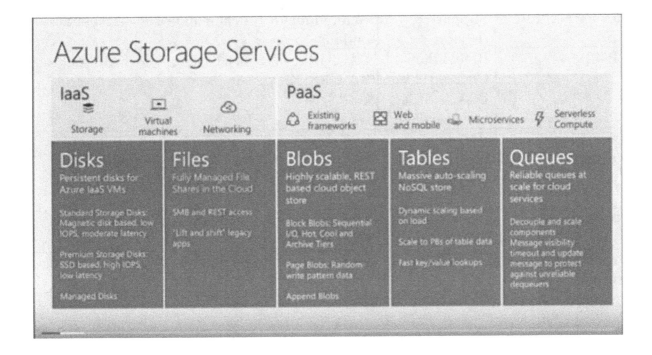

Note: Each of the above Storage service is accessed through a Storage Account. Storage Account will be discussed in next page.

Introduction to Storage Accounts

An Azure storage account provides a unique namespace to store and access your Azure Storage data objects.

Azure Storage (Blob, Table, Queue and Files) is created under Storage Accounts. Storage Account is prerequisite for creating Azure Storage.

Storage Account Performance Tiers

A standard storage performance tier is backed by magnetic disk HDD.
Supports GPv2 Storage Account.

A premium storage performance tier is backed by SSD.
Supports Block Blob Storage, File Storage and Page Storage Account.

Comparing 4 types of Storage Accounts

Storage account type	Supported services	Redundancy options	Performance Tiers	Access tiers
GP-v2	Blob, File, Queue, Table, Disk, and Data Lake Gen.	LRS, GRS, RA-GRS, ZRS, GZRS, RA-GZRS	Standard	Hot, Cool & Archive.
Block Blobs Storage	Blob (block blobs and append blobs only).	LRS, ZRS.	Premium	Hot, Cool & Archive.
File Storage	File Shares only.	LRS, ZRS.	Premium	NA
Page Blobs Storage	Page Blobs	LRS	Premium	NA

Azure Storage Account Replication Options

The data in the Microsoft Azure storage account is always replicated to ensure high availability. **Azure Storage Accounts offer 4 Replication options – LRS, ZRS, GRS & GZRS.**

Locally redundant storage (LRS)

Locally redundant storage (LRS) replicates your data **three times within a datacentre** in which you created your storage account.

Zone-redundant storage (ZRS)

ZRS replicates your data synchronously across **three availability zones (Datacentres) within a region.** ZRS enables customers to read and write data even if a single zone is unavailable or unrecoverable.

Geo Redundant Storage (GRS)

With GRS, data is first replicated 3 times within the **primary region** and then asynchronously replicated to the **secondary region**, where it is also replicated three times.

Geo-zone-redundant storage (GZRS)

Data in a GZRS storage account is copied across three Azure availability zones in the **primary region** and is also replicated to a **secondary geographic region** for protection from regional disasters.

Important Note

With GRS and GZRS you also get the option to read-only access to the data in the secondary location in the event of regional unavailability.

Exercise 7.1: Create Storage Account

In this Exercise we will create Storage Account with name sacloud410 in Resource Group RGCloud and in Region East US 2. Resource Group RGCloud was created in Exercise 4.1 in Chapter 4.

1. Open Chrome Browser and go to Azure Portal @ portal.azure.com> Azure Portal opens as below. In Azure Portal Click 3 Horizontal lines in top left> A pane opens in left of Azure Portal as shown below> Note the Storage accounts option in left pane.

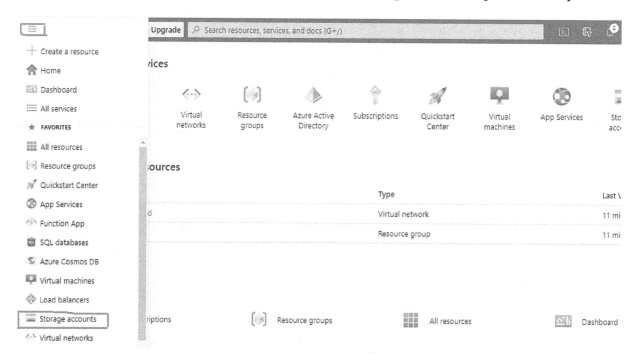

2. In above figure click Storage accounts> All Storage accounts pane opens as shown below> Note the + Create option.

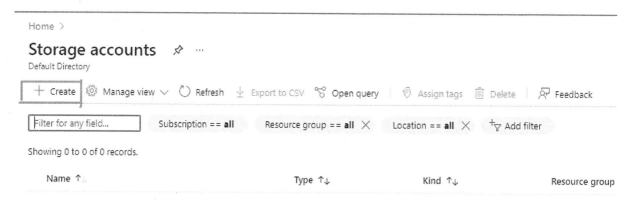

3. In above figure click + Create> Create a storage account blade opens as shown below> In Resource Group select RGCloud> In name I entered saCloud410> In Region select East US 2> For Performance select Standard> For Redundancy select LRS> Click Review + Create> After Validation is passed click Create (Not Shown).

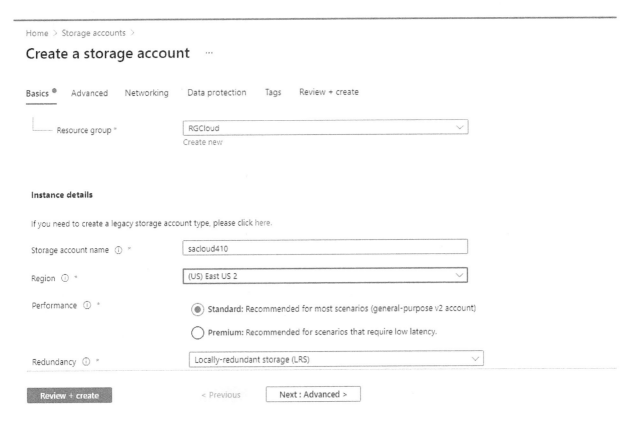

2. Figure below shows the dashboard of Storage account saCloud410. Note the Containers and File shares options. We will use them in upcoming exercises.

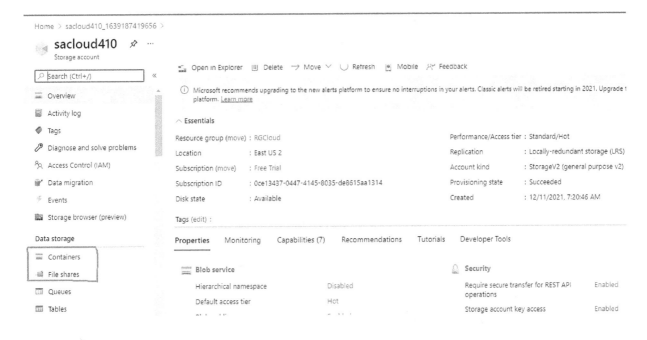

Introduction to Blob Storage

Azure Blob storage stores unstructured data in the cloud as objects/blobs. Azure Blob storage is massively scalable, highly redundant and secure **object storage** with a **URL/http based access** which allows it to be accessed within Azure or outside the Azure. Though Azure objects are regionally scoped you can access them from anywhere in the world.

Blob storage is also referred to as object storage.

Blobs are basically files like those that you store on your computer. They can be pictures, Excel files, HTML files, virtual hard disks (VHDs), log files & database backups etc. Blobs are stored in containers, which are similar to folders. Containers are created under Storage account.

Blob Storage Service Components

Storage Account: All access to Azure Storage is done through a storage account.
Containers: Container is like a folder which store Blob Files.
Blob: A file of any type and size.

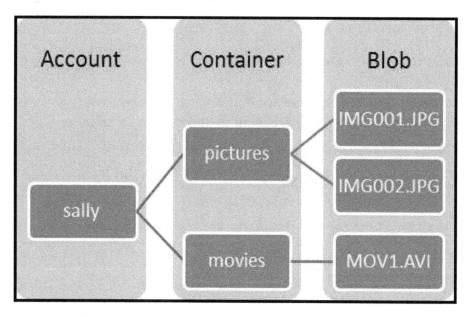

Blob Storage Access Options

Private access: Owner of the Storage Account can access the Blob Data.
Blob (Anonymous read access for Blob only): You can make blobs publicly available for anonymous access.
Container (Anonymous read access for Containers and Blob): You can make a container and blobs publicly available for anonymous access.

Exercise 7.2: Create Blob Storage Container and upload a File

In this exercise we will create Blob Storage Container hk410 in Storage Account sacloud410 and in resource group RGCloud with **anonymous Access.** We will Upload a file to the Blob Container hk410 and access it over internet. Resource group RGCloud was Created in Exercise 4.1 in Chapter 4. Storage Account sacloud410 was created in Exercise 7.1 in this Chapter.

1. In Storage Account sacloud410 Dashboard Click Containers in left pane>All Containers Dashboard opens as shown below> Note the + Container option.

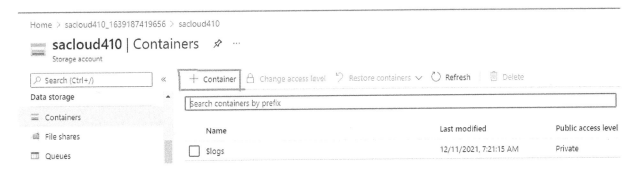

2. In above figure click + Container> Create New Container blade opens as shown below> Enter name **hk410** and select access level **Blob** and click Create (Not Shown).

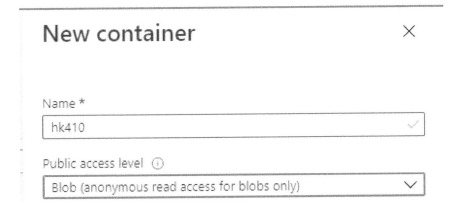

3. Container hk410 (2nd Row) is created as shown in below figure.

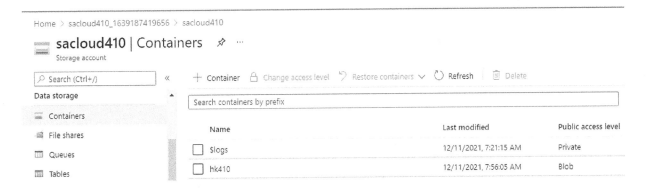

Azure Study & Lab Guide For Beginners

4. **Create a Text file on your Laptop/Desktop:** I created Text file with name helloworld.txt file on my desktop. I also added Hello World ! as content in the file.

5. **Upload a file from your desktop**. In all Container dashboard as shown in Step 3 figure Click the Container hk410>Container hk410 dashboard opens as shown below> In right pane Click Upload> Upload blob blade opens in extreme right>Click file button to upload helloworld.txt file from desktop>Rest keep all values as default>Click Upload> After the file is uploaded close the Upload pane.

6. File is uploaded as shown below. I also clicked … in extreme right to see the option available with uploaded file.

7. In above figure Double click HelloWorld.txt in Container hk410 pane> Blob file helloworld.txt Dashboard opens as shown below>Copy the URL of the file.

8. In Chrome Browser open a browser tab and paste the URL copied from previous step. You can see the contents of the file. We were able to open the file as we had chosen Blob anonymous read permission in step 2. Close the Blob, Container and Storage pane.

Introduction to File Storage

Azure Files Storage offers fully managed file shares in the cloud that are accessible via the industry standard Server Message Block (SMB 3.0) protocol (also known as Common Internet File System or CIFS).

Azure File shares can be mounted concurrently by cloud or on-premises deployments of Windows, Mac OS, and Linux instances.

Figure below shows Multiple Virtual Machines accessing Azure File share.

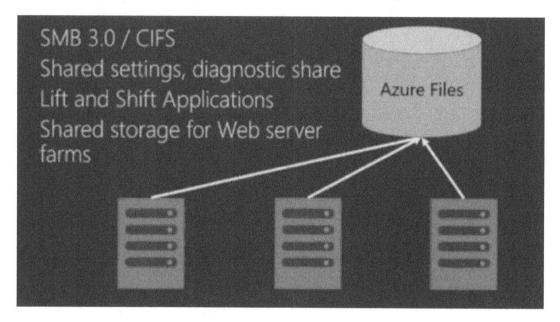

Azure File share Use case

1. Azure Files can be used to completely replace or supplement traditional on-premises file servers or NAS devices.

2. Developers can leverage their existing code and skills to migrate existing applications that rely on file shares to Azure quickly and without costly rewrites.

3. An Azure File share is a convenient place for cloud applications to write their logs, metrics, and crash dumps.

4. When developers or administrators are working on VMs in the cloud, they often need a set of tools or utilities. Copying such utilities and tools to each VM can be a time consuming exercise. By mounting an Azure File share locally on the VMs, a developer and administrator can quickly access their tools and utilities, no copying required.

File Storage Service Architecture and components

Figure below shows the architecture of File share. File share is mounted as a drive on Virtual Machine and is accessed over the network.

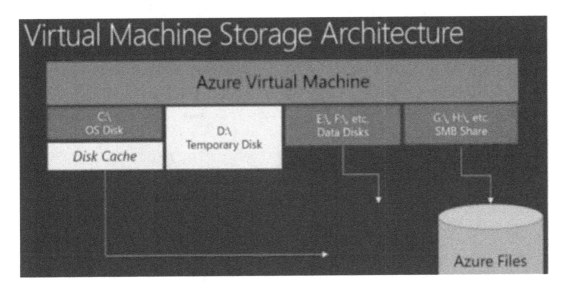

File Service contains 3 components: Storage Account, File Shares and Files.

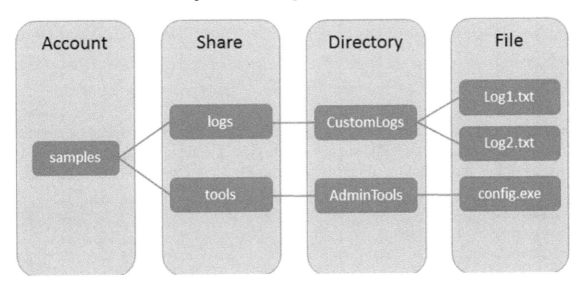

Storage Account: This storage account can be a **GP-v2 or File storage account.**
Share: Share stores the files. Azure File shares can be mounted and accessed concurrently by cloud or on-premises deployments of Windows, Linux, and macOS. A share can store an unlimited number of files.
Directory: Directory is optional. Directory is like a folder for files.
File: A file of any type.

Exercise 7.3: Create and Mount File Share

In this Exercise we will create File Share with name fscloud in Storage account sacloud410 and mount it to Windows VM vmcloud1. Storage Account sacloud410 was created in Exercise 7.1 in this Chapter. VM vmcloud1 was created in Exercise 6.1 in Chapter 6. Make sure VM vmcloud1 is started before you start this Exercise.

1. Go to Storage Account sacloud410 Dashboard> Note the File shares option in left pane.

2. In above figure Click File shares in left pane>File shares dashboard opens as shown below> In right pane Click + File share> Create New file share blade opens in extreme right as shown below>Enter name **fscloud**> Click Create (Not Shown).

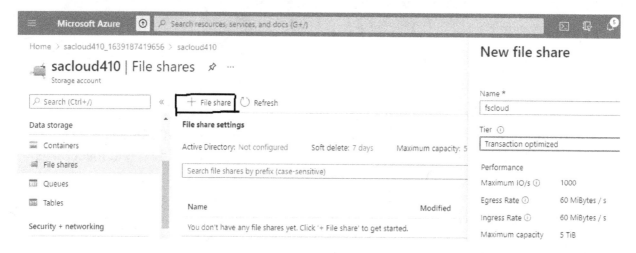

3. Figure below shows File share fscloud in All Files shares pane.

4. In above figure Click File share fscloud> File share fscloud dashboard opens as shown below. Click **Upload** in right pane> Upload files Blade open in extreme right> Click Select a File icon and Upload any file (Text, Word, Excel or Power Point) from your desktop and click upload. After file is uploaded close the upload blade.

5. Back in File share fscloud dashboard you can see the uploaded file> Note the Conect option in right pane.

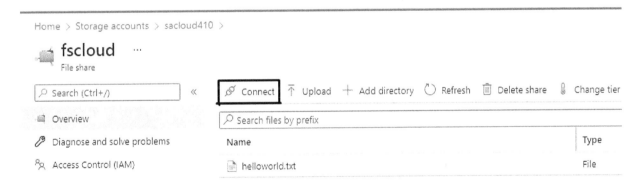

6. In File share fscloud dashboard Click Connect in right pane>Connect Blade opens in extreme right as shown below> Make sure that in Authentication Method Storage account Key option is selected> In rectangular box note the # **Mount the drive** option. Under Mount the drive option you need to copy link appended to double backslashes. In my case it is **sacloud410.file.core.windows.net\fscloud.** Copy this link in Notepad on your Laptop/Desktop. This link will be different in Book Readers case> Close the Connect pane.

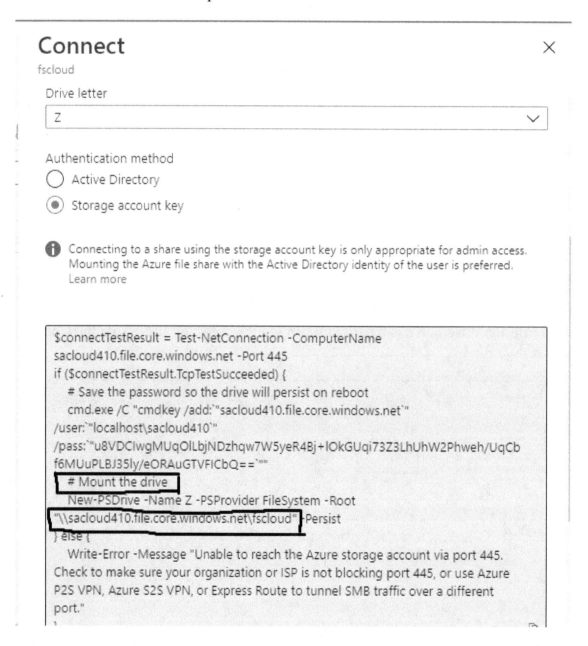

7. Go to Storage Account Dashboard sacloud410 Dashboard>Click Access keys in left pane> In Right pane click Show Keys. Show keys name will now change to Hide Keys> Copy key1 and paste it in Notepad on your laptop/Desktop.

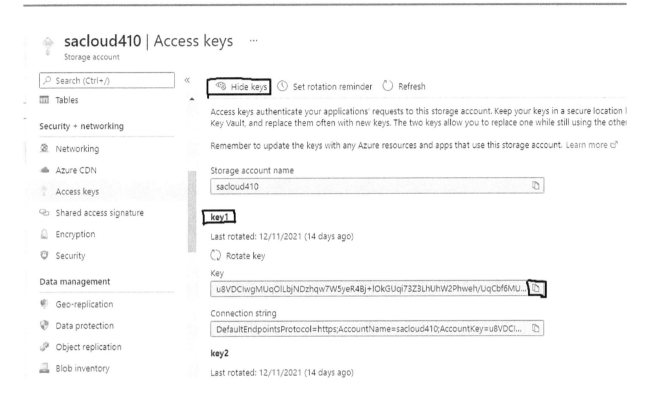

8. **Connect to Azure VM vmcloud1 using RDP.** The Procedure to RDP to VM was shown in Exercise 6.2 in Chapter 6> In VM vmcloud1 RDP pane open File Explorer and click **This PC** in left pane> Note the ⌄ option in Top right in below figure.

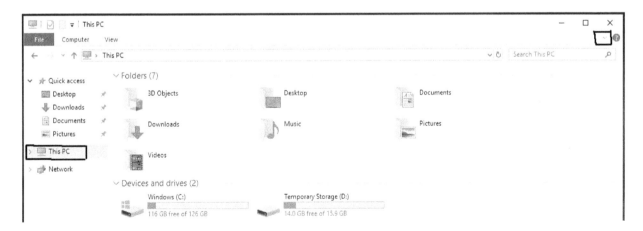

9. In above figure Click ⌄ icon in right side and it opens ribbon items as shown below>
   Note the Map network drive option.

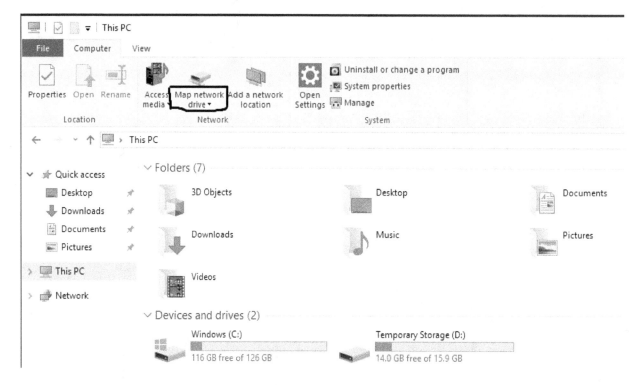

10. In above figure Click Map Network Drive> Click Map Network drive gain. Map
    Network drive blade pops up as shown below> In Folder enter link copied in step 6:
    \\sacloud410.file.core.windows.net\fscloud> Click Finish.

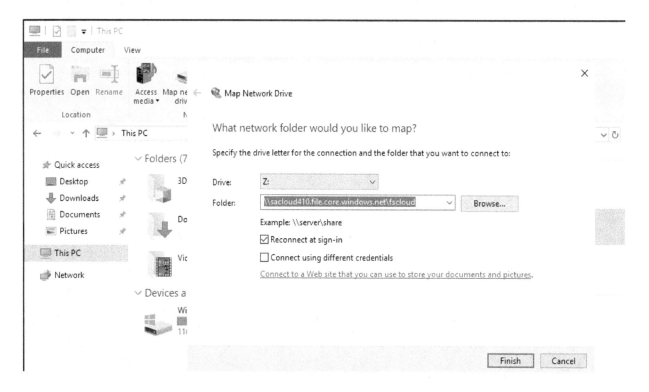

11. Enter network credentials dialog box opens as shown below>In Username enter Storage Account name (sacloud410) prepended with Azure\> In password enter Storage Account sacloud410 Key copied in Step 7> Click Ok.

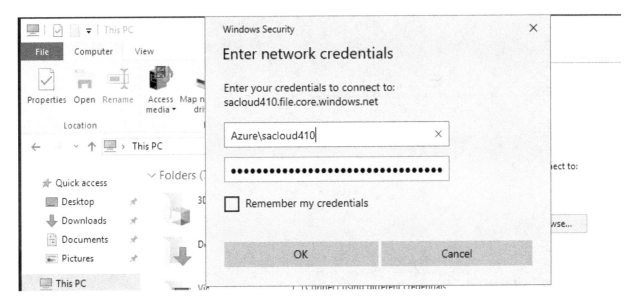

12. Back in Windows Explorer pane you can see that File share fscloud is mounted.

13. In above figure Click on File share fscloud and you can see that HelloWorld.txt file which we had uploaded in step 4.

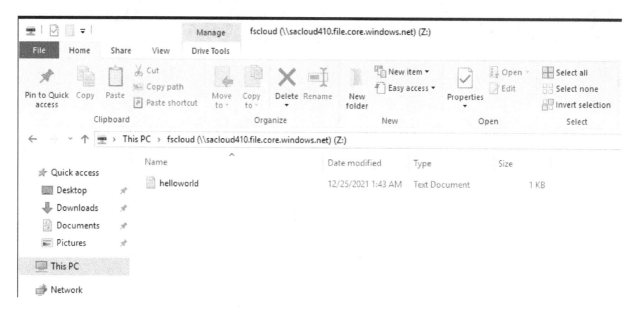

14. Close the VM vmcloud1 RDP pane.
15. Go to VM vmcloud1 dashboard and click Stop in right pane.

Chapter 8 Azure Active Directory

Microsoft Azure Active Directory or Azure AD is a Multi-tenant cloud-based directory & identity management solution that combines core directory services, application access management, and identity protection into a single solution.

Azure AD also provides enterprise service's such as multifactor authentication service, a centralized application access panel for SaaS applications, an application proxy by which you can setup remote access for your on premises applications as well as Graph API that you can use to directly interact with Azure AD objects.

One of the Advantage of Azure AD is that application developers can easily integrate identity management in their application without writing complex code.

Azure AD can also act as Identity provider. It Provides identity and authentication services to application using SAML, WS-Federation and OpenID connect protocols.

Azure Active Directory editions

Azure AD is offered in 4 Tiers: Free, Basic, Premium P1, Premium P2

Azure Active Directory Free edition can manage users and groups, synchronize with on-premises directories, get single sign-on across Azure, Office 365, and thousands of popular SaaS applications.

Office 365 App Edition adds features such as group-based access management, self-service password reset for cloud applications, and Azure Active Directory Application Proxy. Office 365 App Edition comes bundled with Office 365.

Azure Active Directory Premium P1 edition add enterprise class features such as enhanced monitoring & security reporting, Multi-Factor Authentication (MFA), and secure access for your mobile workforce.

Azure Active Directory Premium P2 edition adds Identity Protection and Privileged Identity Management features.

Comparing Azure AD Editions

Features	Free	Office 365 App	Premium (P1 & P2)
Directory Objects	50000	No Limit	No Limit
User/Group Management	√	√	√
Single sign-on (SSO)	10 apps/user	10 apps/user	No limit
Self-Service Password Change for cloud users	√	√	√
AD Connect	√	√	√
Security/Usage Reports	3 Basic Reports	3 Basic Reports	Advanced Reports
Multi Factor Authentication for Administrator Roles	√	√	√
Group based access Management		√	√
Self Service password reset for cloud users		√	√
Logon page customization		√	√
SLA 99.9%		√	√
Multi Factor Authentication		√	√
Advanced Self Service Group and app management including Dynamic Groups			√
Self Service Password reset with on premises write back			√
Azure AD Join (MDM & Enterprise State Roaming)			√
Microsoft Identity Manager user CAL + MIM Server			√
Azure AD Connect Health			√
Application Proxy			√
Conditional Access			√
Identity Protection			Premium P2
Privileged Identity Management			Premium P2
Access Reviews			Premium P2
Pricing	**Free**	**Included with O365**	**P1- $6 user/month** **P2- $9 user/month**

Important Note Regarding Office 365 App Edition: Office 365 App Edition comes bundled with Office 365.

Exercise 8.1: Accessing Default Azure AD Tenant

A Default Azure AD Tenant Free Edition is automatically created with the subscription. You can upgrade Default Free edition to Premium Edition.

Domain name of the default Azure AD is in the following format:
<System generated Name>.onmicrosoft.com

System generated Name is based on the name and mail id used to create the subscription. You can check default Azure AD by going to Azure AD Dashboard. Figure below shows dashboard of default Azure AD Tenant **sk41087outlook.onmicrosoft.com** which I am using for this book.

1. Open Chrome Browser and log on to Azure Portal @ portal.azure.com using Subscription Administrator credentials> Azure Portal opens. In Azure Portal Click 3 Horizontal lines in top left> A pane opens in left of Azure Portal> Note the Azure Active Directory option in left pane.

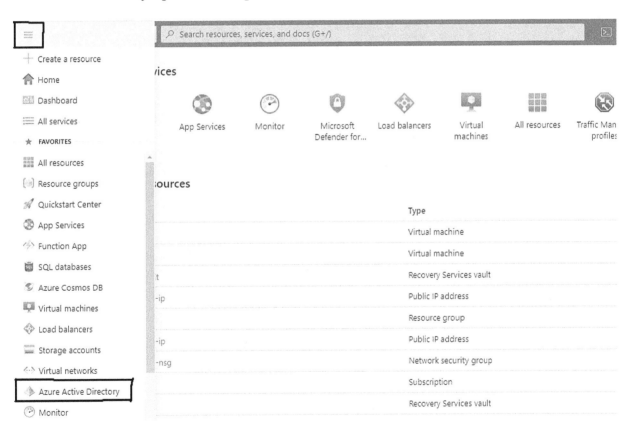

2. In above figure Click Azure Active Directory option in left pane> Dashboard of
    default Azure AD Tenant **sk41087outlook.onmicrosoft.com opens as shown
    below**> Note the Users and Groups options in left pane. We will use them to create
    Users and Groups in upcoming Exercises

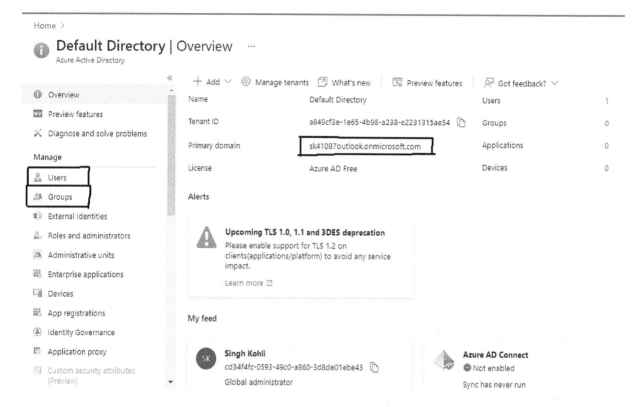

Note: Azure AD User name should be in email format with a verified domain. Verified
domain can be default domain or custom Domain. User login name for the above default
domain will be **xyzxyz@sk41087outlook.onmicrosoft.com.**

Azure AD Users

Users in Azure AD can be of following types:

1. Cloud User. Exists in Azure AD only.
2. Guest User or B2B user. B2B user exists outside of Azure AD.
3. Users Synchronized from On-Premises Active Directory to Azure AD using AD Connect.

Directory Role for Users

User is assigned Directory role during user creation time. A user can be assigned one of the following 3 directory roles:

User: User role option has Read Access to Azure AD.
Global Administrator: The Global administrators have full access to Azure Active Directory (Azure AD) resources only.
Limited Administrator: Limited administrator role has full access to particular feature of Azure AD. Following are some of the Limited Administrative roles available in Azure.
Note: There is no Role with name Limited Administrator.

Billing Administrator	Exchange Service Administrator	Password Administrator / Helpdesk Administrator
Compliance Administrator	Global Administrator / Company Administrator	Power BI Service Administrator
Conditional Access Administrator	Guest Inviter	Privileged Role Administrator
Dynamics 365 service administrator	Information Protection Administrator	Security Administrator

Very Important Point: For Global Administrator, Limited Administrator & Users to manage or create Azure resources they must be assigned permissions using Role based Access Control (RBAC).

Exercise 8.2: Create Azure AD User (User1 with Global Administrator Role)

1. In Chrome Browser while logged on with Subscription Administrator credentials, Go to Azure AD Dashboard as shown in Exercise 8.1> Click Users in left pane> All Users blade opens as shown below> Note the + New user option> Note the User Singh Kohli. This was the name with which I signed for Azure Subscription. In Book Readers case it will be the name with which they signed Azure Trial Subscription.

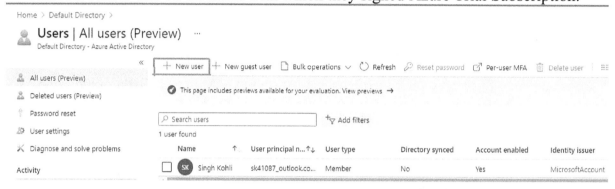

2. In above figure Click +New user> Add New user blade opens as shown below> Make sure Create User radio button is selected (Not shown)>In User name enter **user1**> In Name Enter **User1**> Under **Password** select **Let me create the password** and then enter password> Note the link User. In next step we will use this link to assign Global Administrator Role to User1.

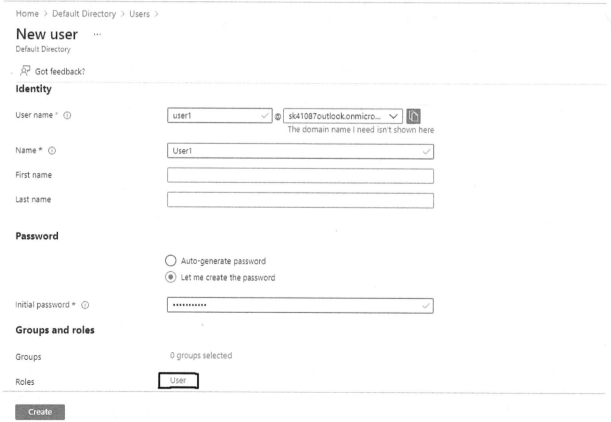

3. In above figure click link **User**> Directory roles pane opens in right side as shown below>In Directory role pane Scroll down and select Global administrator and click select (Not shown).

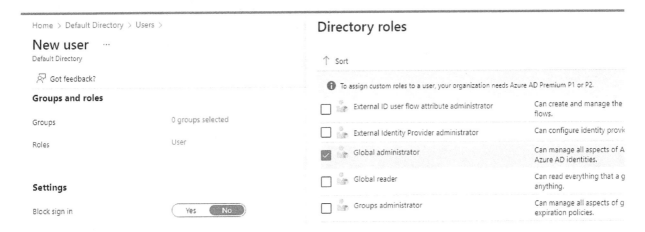

Note: By default User is assigned Directory role of User.

4. You can see in below figure that Azure AD User User1 is assigned Directory Role of Global Administrator. Click **Create.**

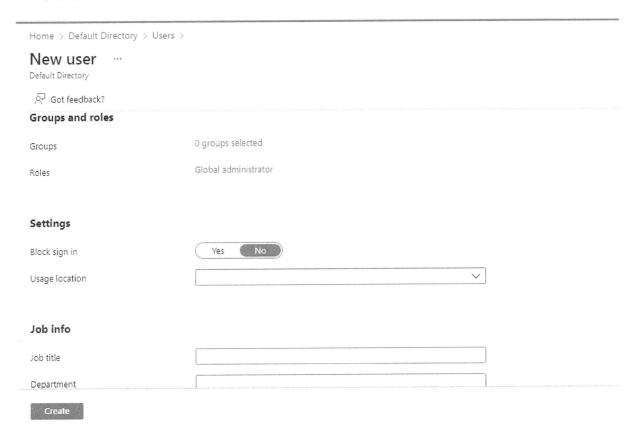

Important Note: In Step 2 you can see user name option. It shows user1@sk41087outlook.onmicrosoft.com. This is User1 login name for Azure Portal.

5. All Users pane opens as shown below> You can see that User1 is created (2nd Row). User1 login name to Azure Portal is mentioned under User principal name (2nd Column). In my case it is **user1@sk41087outlook.onmicrosoft.com.** <u>In Book Readers case User1 login name will be different. Instead of sk41087outlook (System generated name) they will have different System generated name.</u>

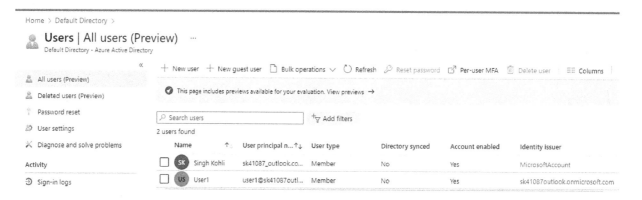

6. Open **Firefox** and go to Azure Portal @ https://portal azure.com and Log on with User1 Credentials (user1@sk41087outlook.onmicrosoft.com) and Password you entered in step 2> System will ask you to change the password as you have logged on for first time> Azure Portal now opens as shown below.

Figure below shows Azure Portal for User1. **User1 has no access to Azure Resources nor can it create any resources.** I tried to create Azure VM but was not able to create it. **It only has full access to Azure AD as User1 is Global Administrator.** It can create Users and Groups.

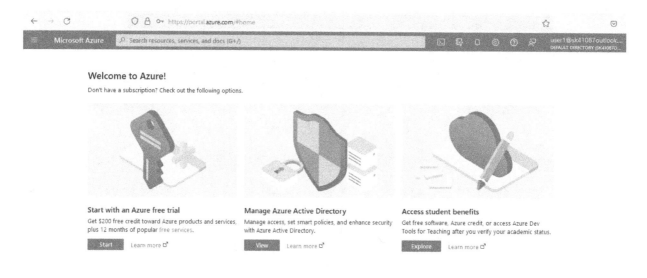

7. Still in Firefox Browser Click 3 Horizontal lines in top left> A pane opens in left of Azure Portal> Click Azure Active Directory option in left pane> Dashboard of default Azure AD Tenant **sk41087outlook.onmicrosoft.com opens as shown below>** As User1 is Global Administrator it has full access to Azure AD only. It can also create Users and Groups.

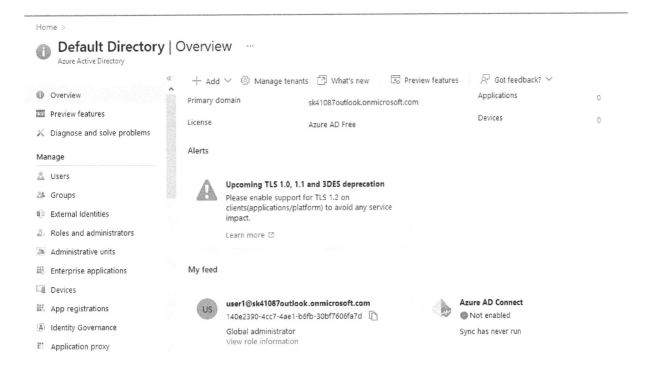

8. In Firefox Logout User1 from Azure portal by clicking Profile icon in top right and then clicking sign out.

Note: Azure AD Users access to Azure resource requires Role based Access control (RBAC). RBAC will be discussed in next Chapter.

Exercise 8.3: Create Azure AD User (User2 with User Role)

1. In Chrome Browser while logged on with Subscription Administrator credentials, Go to Azure AD Dashboard as shown in Exercise 8.1> Click Users in left pane> All Users blade opens as shown below> Note the + New user option.

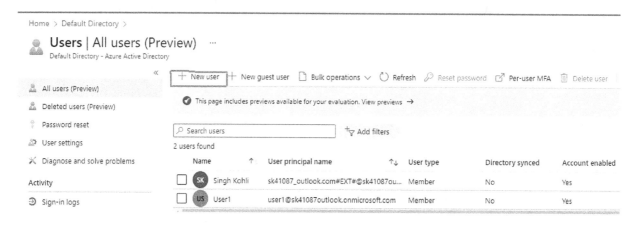

2. In above figure Click +New user> Add New user blade opens as shown below> Make sure Create User radio button is selected> In User name enter **user2**> In Name Enter **User2**.

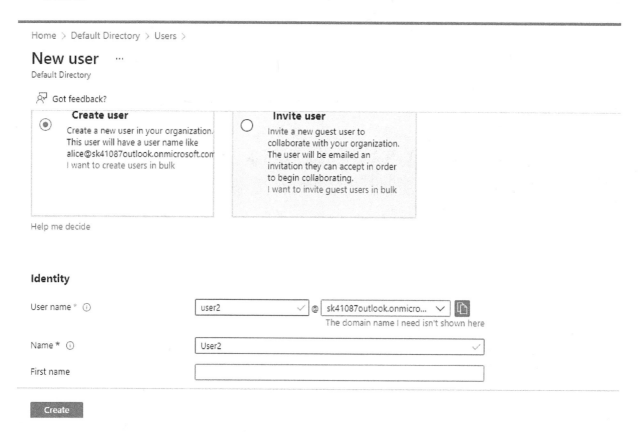

3. Scroll down in above figure> Under **Password** select **Let me create the password** and then enter password> Click Create. By default User is assigned Directory Role of User.

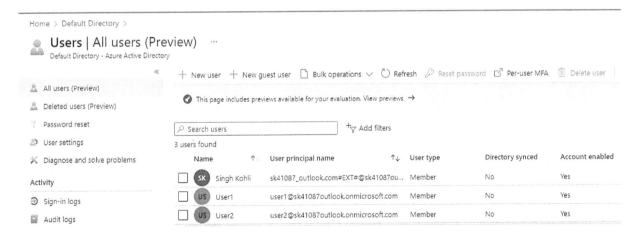

Home > Default Directory > Users >

New user   ...
Default Directory

⟨⟩ Got feedback?

Password

○ Auto-generate password
◉ Let me create the password

Initial password * ⓘ   ⬤⬤⬤⬤⬤⬤⬤⬤⬤⬤⬤   ✓

Groups and roles

Groups   0 groups selected

Roles   User

Settings

Block sign in   Yes   **No**

Create

4. All Users pane opens as shown below> You can see that User2 is created (3rd Row). User2 login name to Azure Portal is mentioned under User principal name (2nd Column). In my case it is **user2@sk41087outlook.onmicrosoft.com.** In Book Readers case User2 login name will be different. Instead of sk41087outlook (System generated name) they will have different System generated name.

Home > Default Directory >

Users | All users (Preview)   ...
Default Directory - Azure Active Directory

《   + New user   + New guest user   ☐ Bulk operations ∨   ○ Refresh   ⟨ Reset password   ☐ Per-user MFA   🗑 Delete user

All users (Preview)
Deleted users (Preview)   ⓘ This page includes previews available for your evaluation. View previews →

Password reset
User settings   🔍 Search users   ⊤ Add filters
Diagnose and solve problems   3 users found

	Name ↑	User principal name ↑↓	User type	Directory synced	Account enabled
Activity | ☐ SK Singh Kohli | sk41087_outlook.com#EXT#@sk41087ou... | Member | No | Yes |
Sign-in logs | ☐ US User1 | user1@sk41087outlook.onmicrosoft.com | Member | No | Yes |
Audit logs | ☐ US User2 | user2@sk41087outlook.onmicrosoft.com | Member | No | Yes |

5. Open **Firefox** and go to Azure Portal @ https://portal azure.com and Log on with User2 Credentials (user2@sk41087outlook.onmicrosoft.com) and Password you entered in step 3> System will ask you to change the password as you have logged on for first time> Azure Portal now opens as shown below.

Figure below shows Azure Portal for User2. **User2 has no access to Azure Resources nor can it create any resources.** I tried to create Azure VM but was not able to create it. **It only has <u>Read access</u> to Azure AD as User2 has Directory Role of User.** User2 can't create Users and Groups.

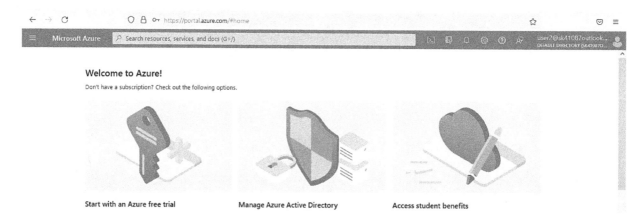

6. Still in Firefox Browser Click 3 Horizontal lines in top left> A pane opens in left of Azure Portal> Click Azure Active Directory option in left pane> Dashboard of default Azure AD Tenant opens as shown below. Scroll down in right pane and you can see User2 is assigned Directory Role of User.

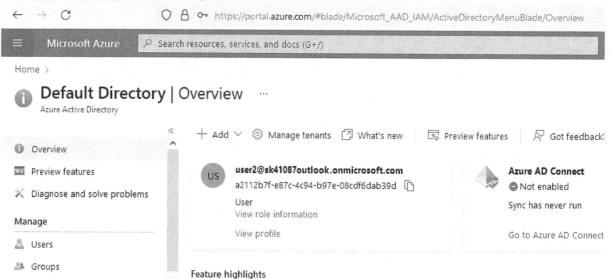

7. In Firefox Logout User2 from Azure portal by clicking Profile icon in top right and then clicking sign out.
   Note: Azure AD Users access to Azure resource requires Role based Access control (RBAC). RBAC will be discussed in next Chapter.

Exercise 8.4: Create Azure AD User (User3 with User Role)

1. In Chrome Browser while logged on with Subscription Administrator credentials, Go to Azure AD Dashboard as shown in Exercise 8.1> Click Users in left pane> All Users blade opens as shown below> Note the + New user option.

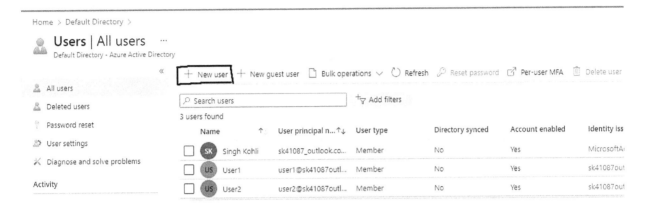

2. In above figure Click +New user> Add New user blade opens as shown below> Make sure Create User radio button is selected> In User name enter **user3**> In Name Enter **User3**.

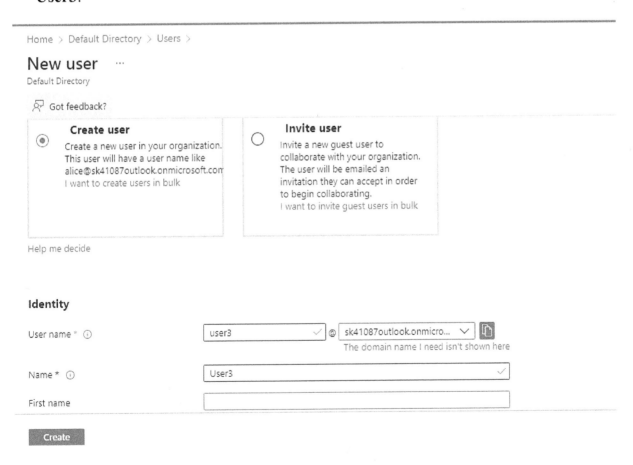

3. Scroll down in above figure> Under **Password** select **Let me create the password** and then enter password> Click Create. By default User is assigned Directory Role of User.

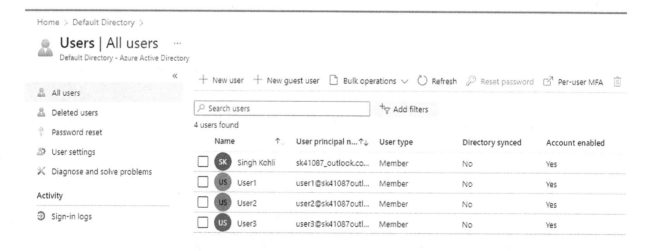

Home > Default Directory > Users >

New user ...
Default Directory

🖉 Got feedback?

○ Auto-generate password
◉ Let me create the password

Initial password * ⓘ   ············ ✓

Groups and roles

Groups   0 groups selected

Roles   User

Settings

Block sign in   Yes **No**

Usage location   ⌄

[Create]

4. All Users pane opens as shown below> You can see that User3 is created (4th Row). User3 login name to Azure Portal is mentioned under User principal name (2nd Column). In my case it is **user3@sk41087outlook.onmicrosoft.com.** In Book Readers case User3 login name will be different. Instead of sk41087outlook (System generated name) they will have different System generated name.

Home > Default Directory >

Users | All users ...
Default Directory - Azure Active Directory

+ New user   + New guest user   ▢ Bulk operations ⌄   ↻ Refresh   🔑 Reset password   ⬈ Per-user MFA 🗑

All users

Deleted users   🔍 Search users   ⁺▽ Add filters

Password reset   4 users found

User settings

Diagnose and solve problems

Activity

Sign-in logs

Name			User principal n... ↑↓	User type	Directory synced	Account enabled
☐	SK	Singh Kohli	sk41087_outlook.co...	Member	No	Yes
☐	US	User1	user1@sk41087outl...	Member	No	Yes
☐	US	User2	user2@sk41087outl...	Member	No	Yes
☐	US	User3	user3@sk41087outl...	Member	No	Yes

5. Open **Firefox** and go to Azure Portal @ https://portal azure.com and Log on with User3 Credentials (user3@sk41087outlook.onmicrosoft.com) and Password you entered in step 3> System will ask you to change the password as you have logged on for first time> Azure Portal now opens as shown below.

Figure below shows Azure Portal for User3. **User3 has no access to Azure Resources nor can it create any resources.** I tried to create Azure VM but was not able to create it. **It only has <u>Read access</u> to Azure AD as User3 has Directory Role of User.** User3 can't create Users and Groups.

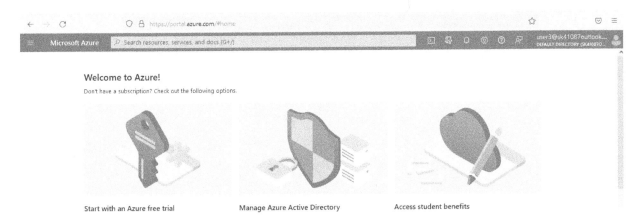

6. Still in Firefox Browser Click 3 Horizontal lines in top left> A pane opens in left of Azure Portal> Click Azure Active Directory option in left pane> Dashboard of default Azure AD Tenant opens as shown below. Scroll down in right pane and you can see User3 is assigned Directory Role of User.

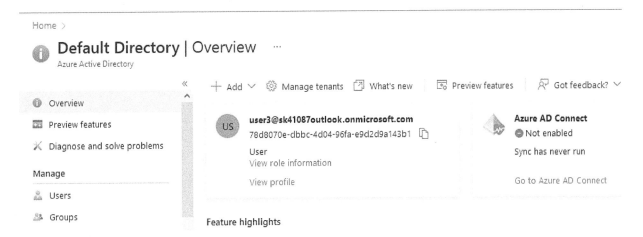

7. In Firefox Logout User3 from Azure portal by clicking Profile icon in top right and then clicking sign out.
Note: Azure AD Users access to Azure resource requires Role based Access control (RBAC). RBAC will be discussed in next Chapter.

Exercise 8.5: Check Profile of Azure AD User User2

In this Exercise we will check Profile of Azure AD User User2. Azure AD User User2 was created in Exercise 8.3 in this Chapter.

1. In Chrome Browser while logged on with Subscription Administrator credentials, Go to Azure AD Dashboard as shown in Exercise 7.1> Click Users in left pane> All Users blade opens as shown below. Note User2 (3rd Row).

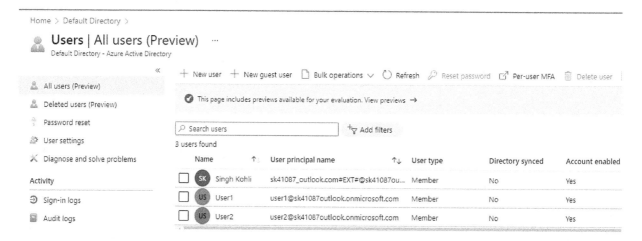

2. In above figure click User2> User2 Profile pane opens as shown below. Readers are requested to scroll down in right pane and study all options. Readers are also requested to click options in left pane and study them.

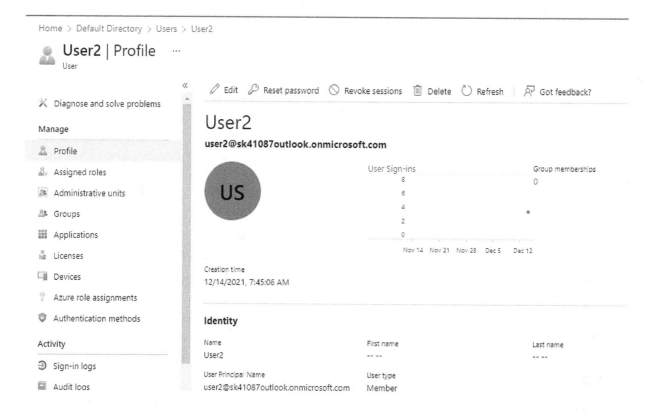

Exercise 8.6: Check Available Azure AD Built-in Roles

1. In Chrome Browser while logged on with Subscription Administrator credentials, Go to Azure AD Dashboard as shown in Exercise 8.1> Click **Roles and administrators** in left pane > In right pane you can see list of available Roles> Scroll down to see more Azure AD Roles.

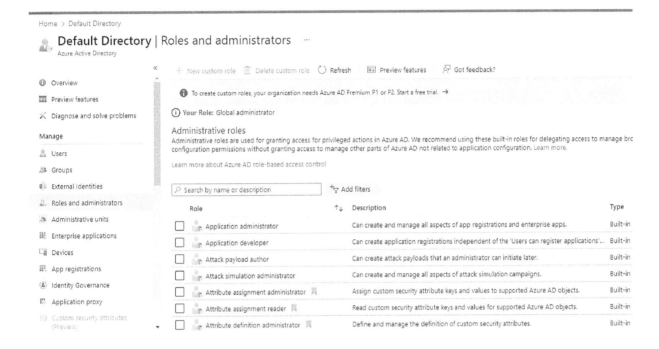

Exercise 8.7: Check Directory Roles Assigned to Azure AD User (User2)

In this Exercise we will check Directory Roles Assigned to Azure AD User User2. Azure AD User User2 was created in Exercise 8.3 in this Chapter.

1. In Chrome Browser while logged on with Subscription Administrator credentials, Go to Azure AD Dashboard as shown in Exercise 7.1> Click Users in left pane> All Users blade opens as shown below. Note User2 (3rd Row).

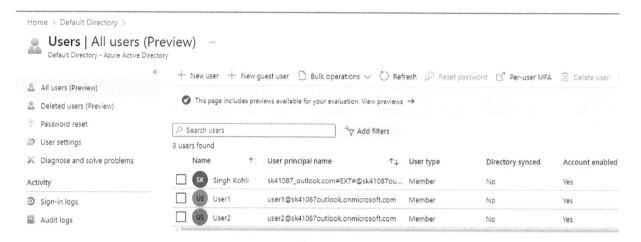

2. In above figure click User2> User2 Profile pane opens as shown below> Click Assigned roles in left pane. In right pane you can see that currently no Administrative roles are assigned to User2.

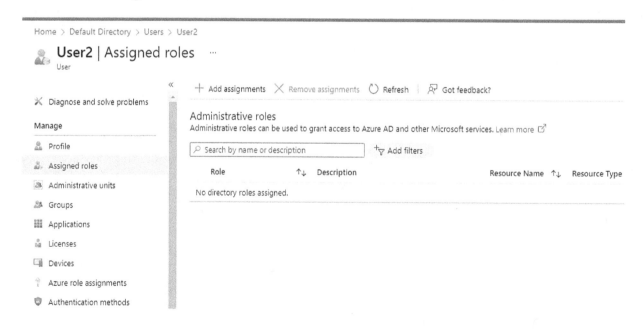

Exercise 8.8: Assign Directory Role of Billing Admin to Azure AD User User2

In this Exercise we will Assign Directory Role of Billing Administrator to Azure AD User User2. Azure AD User User2 was created in Exercise 8.3 in this Chapter.

1. In above figure click + Add assignments in right pane> Directory roles pane opens in extreme right as shown below> Scroll down in Directory roles pane till you see Billing administrator Role as shown below> Select Billing administrator> Click Add.

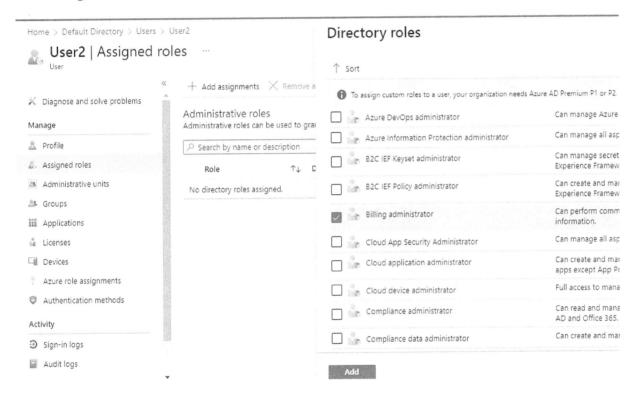

2. You will be back in Assigned roles pane> Click Refresh in right pane and you can see Directory role of Billing administrator assigned to User2.

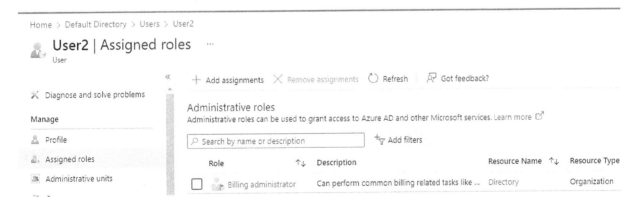

Exercise 8.9: Resetting User Password

Assuming that User2 has forgotten its password and Self Service Password Reset (SSPR) is not enabled. In this case Subscription Administrator or any other Global Administrator can reset User2 password. Azure AD User User2 was created in Exercise 8.3.

1. In Chrome Browser while logged on with Subscription Administrator credentials, Go to Azure AD Dashboard as shown in Exercise 8.1> In Azure AD Dashboard Click Users in left pane>All Users pane opens> Click User2. User2 Profile pane opens as shown below. Note the Reset password option in right pane.

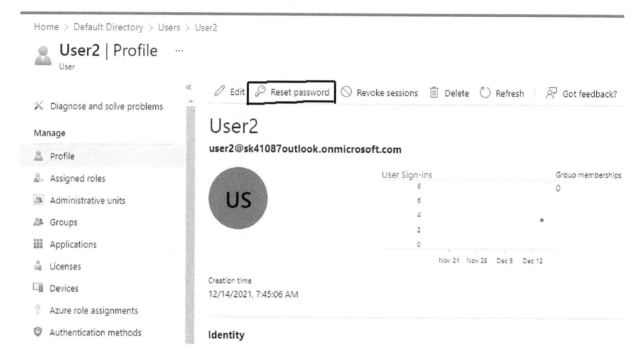

2. In above figure Click Reset password > Reset password pane opens as shown below.

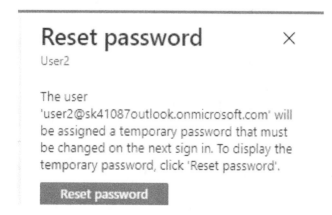

3. Click Reset Password in above figure>A temporary password is displayed as shown below> Copy this password.

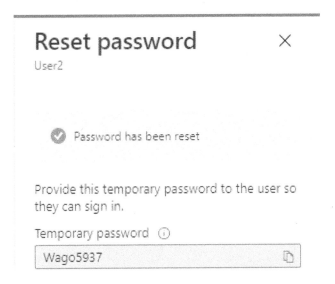

4. Open **Firefox** and log-on to Azure Portal (portal.azure.com) with User2 credentials **(user2@sk41087outlook.onmicrosoft.com)** and temporary password you copied in previous step> Update password pane opens as shown below> Enter your temporary password followed by your new password> User2 is now logged on to Azure Portal.

5. In Firefox Logout User2 from Azure Portal.

Exercise 8.10: Activating Premium P2 Free Trial Licenses

In Azure Portal you get 2 options to activate Premium P2 Free Trial Licenses.

One option is Enterprise Mobility + Security E5 option which includes Azure Active Directory Premium P2, Microsoft Intune and Azure Rights Management Trial Licenses for 250 users for 90 days.
Second Option is Azure AD Premium P2 trial licenses for 100 users for 30 days.

In this exercise we will activate Premium P2 Free Trial Licenses using Enterprise Mobility + Security E5 option.

1. In Chrome Browser while logged on with Subscription Administrator credentials, Go to Azure AD Dashboard as shown in Exercise 8.1> In Azure AD Dashboard Click Licenses in left pane> Licenses Pane opens as shown below> In licenses Dashboard note the option **Get a free trial** under Quick tasks.

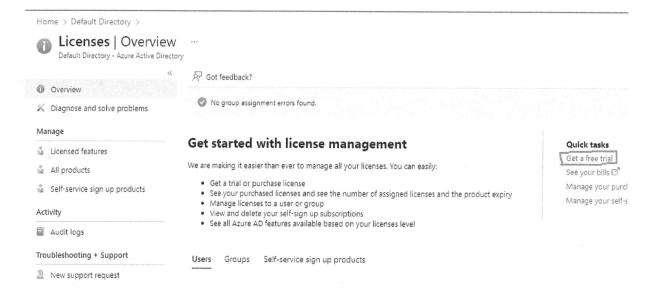

Note: Readers are requested to Activate Enterprise Mobility + Security E5 option only. With Enterprise Mobility + Security E5 option you get 90 days trial licenses instead of 30 Days with Premium P2 option.

2. In above figure Click link **Get a free trial>** Activate Pane opens as shown below> Under Enterprise Mobility + Security E5 option expand Free trial by Clicking Free trial> Note the Activate option.

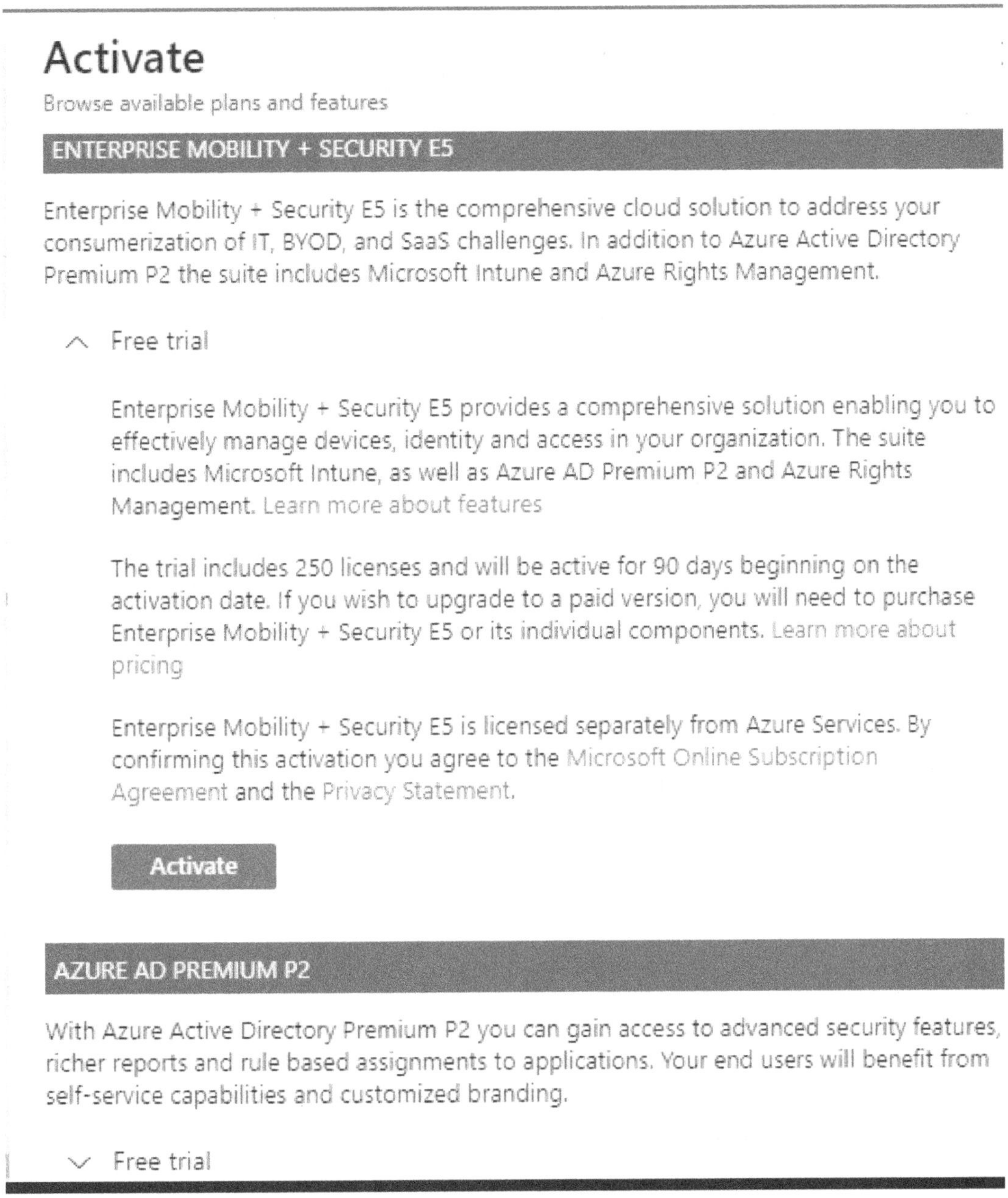

Activate
Browse available plans and features

ENTERPRISE MOBILITY + SECURITY E5

Enterprise Mobility + Security E5 is the comprehensive cloud solution to address your consumerization of IT, BYOD, and SaaS challenges. In addition to Azure Active Directory Premium P2 the suite includes Microsoft Intune and Azure Rights Management.

∧ Free trial

Enterprise Mobility + Security E5 provides a comprehensive solution enabling you to effectively manage devices, identity and access in your organization. The suite includes Microsoft Intune, as well as Azure AD Premium P2 and Azure Rights Management. Learn more about features

The trial includes 250 licenses and will be active for 90 days beginning on the activation date. If you wish to upgrade to a paid version, you will need to purchase Enterprise Mobility + Security E5 or its individual components. Learn more about pricing

Enterprise Mobility + Security E5 is licensed separately from Azure Services. By confirming this activation you agree to the Microsoft Online Subscription Agreement and the Privacy Statement.

Activate

AZURE AD PREMIUM P2

With Azure Active Directory Premium P2 you can gain access to advanced security features, richer reports and rule based assignments to applications. Your end users will benefit from self-service capabilities and customized branding.

∨ Free trial

3. In above figure Click Activate> In 1-2 seconds you will get notification - Successfully activated **Enterprise Mobility + Security E5 trial**> You need to click the notification icon to see the notification.

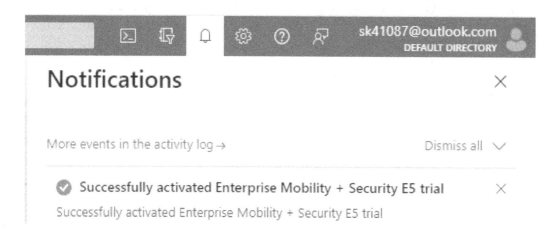

4. In Azure AD licenses pane Click All Products in left pane> you can see that 250 Enterprise Mobility + Security E5 licenses are available. None of the license is assigned> Close the License pane.

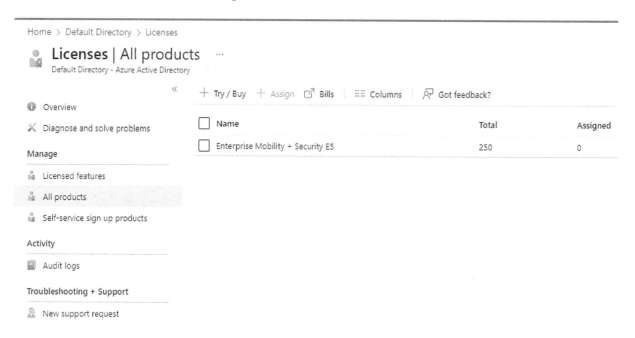

Azure AD Groups

Group is a collection of users. The advantage of Group is that it lowers administrative overhead of managing users. For Example instead of assigning Azure AD premium licenses to individual users, assign it to group.

Using Groups lets the resource owner (or Azure AD directory owner), assign a set of access permissions to all the members of the group, instead of having to provide the rights one-by-one.

Adding Users to Group

Users can be added to group by **manual selection** or by using **dynamic membership rules**.

Membership types in Groups

Assigned: Lets you manually add users to be members of the group.

Dynamic user: Lets you use dynamic membership rules to automatically add and remove users. If a user attributes change, the system looks at your dynamic group rules for the directory to see if the member meets the rule requirements (is added) or no longer meets the rules requirements (is removed).

Dynamic device: Lets you use dynamic group rules to automatically add and remove devices. If a device's attributes change, the system looks at your dynamic group rules for the directory to see if the device meets the rule requirements (is added) or no longer meets the rules requirements (is removed).

Types of Groups

Security Group: Security groups can contain users or devices. It is used to manage Azure AD User and computer access to resources in Azure AD.

Office 365 Group: It is used manage members access to resources in Office 365/Microsoft 365.

Exercise 8.11: Create Group and add Users manually

In this lab we will create Azure AD Group **AZ-MG** and add 3 users (Singh Kohli, User1 & User2) to the group Manually. **Singh Kohli is the user with which we created Azure Subscription.** In Book Readers case it will be your name with you created Azure Trial Subscription. Azure AD Users User1 & User2 were created in Exercise 8.2 & 8.3.

1. In Chrome Browser while logged on with Subscription Administrator credentials, Go to Azure AD Dashboard as shown in Exercise 8.1> Azure AD Dashboard opens as shown below> Note the Groups option in left pane.

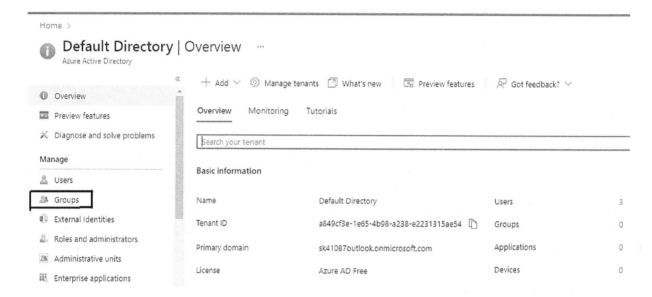

2. In Azure AD Dashboard Click Groups in left pane>All Groups pane opens as shown below> Note the New group option in right pane.

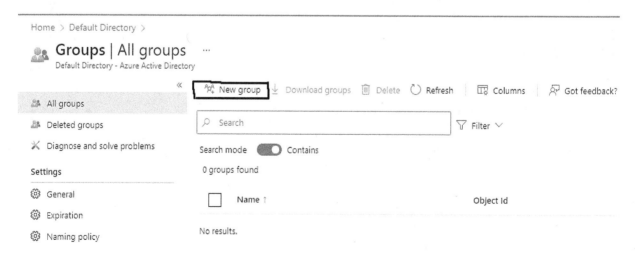

3. In above Click New Group> Add Group Blade opens as shown below>Select Group
type as Security>For Group name enter **AZ-MZ**> Optionally Enter Group
Description> For Azure AD roles can be assigned to the group select the default No
option> Select Membership type **Assigned>** Note the Link **No members selected.**
We will use this link to add Azure AD Users in next step.

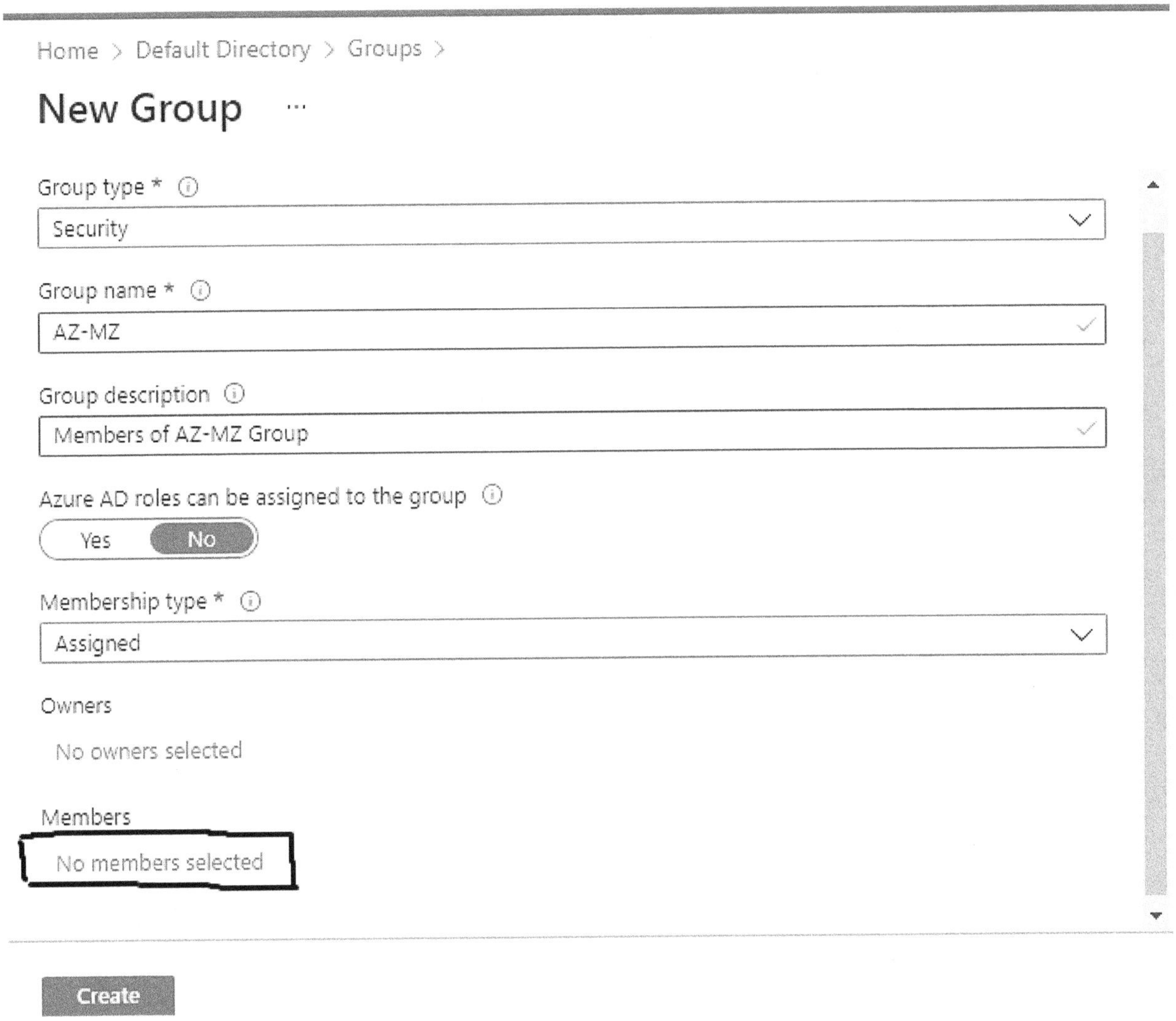

Home > Default Directory > Groups >

New Group   ...

Group type * ⓘ

Security	⌄

Group name * ⓘ

AZ-MZ	✓

Group description ⓘ

Members of AZ-MZ Group	✓

Azure AD roles can be assigned to the group ⓘ

(Yes **No**)

Membership type * ⓘ

Assigned	⌄

Owners

No owners selected

Members

No members selected

Create

4. In above figure under Members click the link **No member selected**> Add members pane opens as shown below> > In search pane enter User and in search result select User1, User2 & User3 and they will appear under Selected Items as shown below> In search pane enter Singh and in search result select Singh Kohli and Singh Kohli will appear under Selected Items. <u>In Book Readers case they need to search for name with which they signed for Trial Subscription</u>> Click Select.

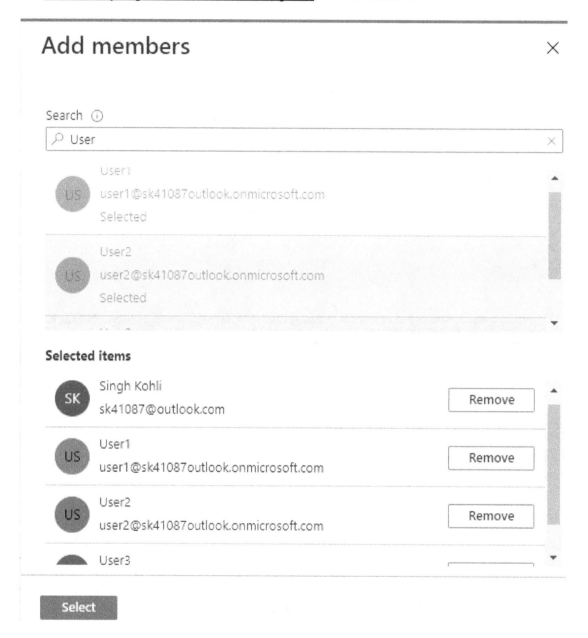

5. Back in create New Group pane you can see 4 Members selected> Click Create.

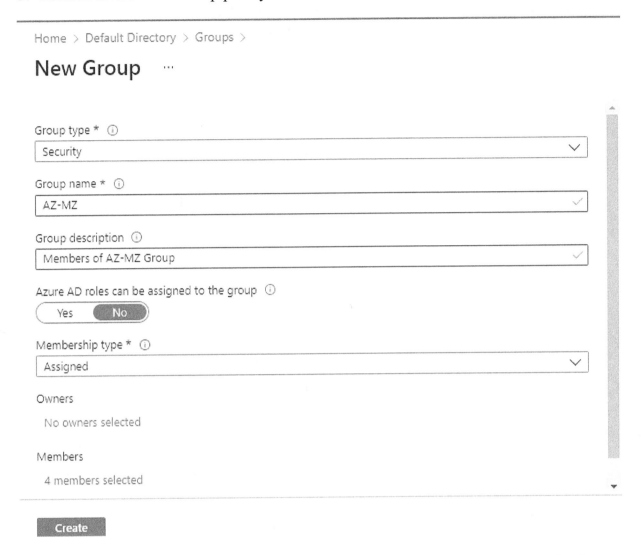

6. Figure below shows AZ-MZ Group in All Groups pane. If required press Refresh.

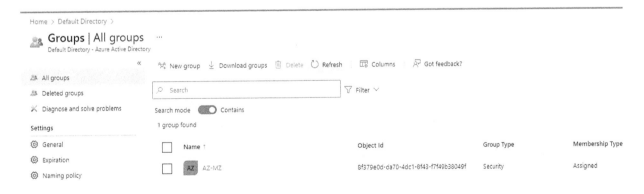

7. In above figure Click AZ-MZ Group and AZ-MZ group dashboard opens as shown below> Note the **Licenses** option in left pane. In next exercise we will use this option to assign Enterprise Mobility + Security E5 license to AZ-MZ Group.

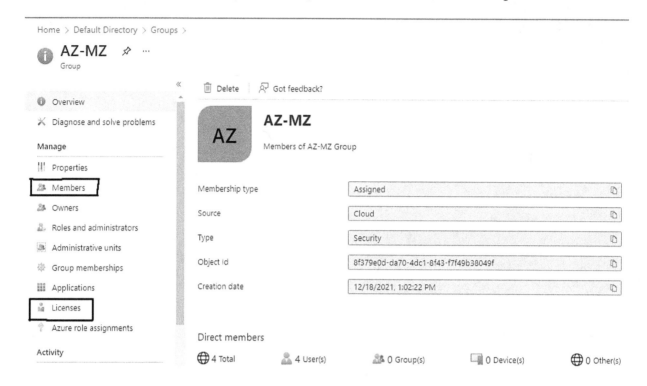

8. In above figure Click Members in left pane> You can see the 4 Members of the Group.

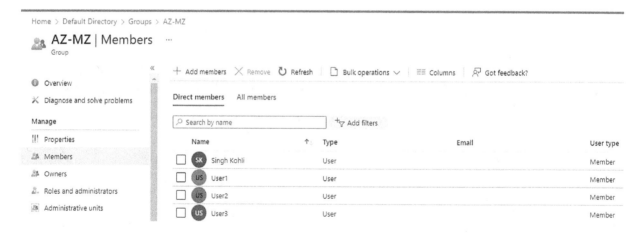

Note: Readers are requested to explore other options in Group Dashboard including the Properties option.

Exercise 8.12: Assigning Enterprise Mobility + Security E5 License to Group

In this exercise we will assign Enterprise Mobility + Security E5 license to users. Instead of assigning Licenses to users individually we will assign licenses to AZ-MZ group created in previous exercise. AZ-MZ Group consists of Singh Kohli, User1, User2 & User3 as members. In Book readers case Singh Kohli will be replaced by the name with which they signed for Azure Trial Subscription.

1. In Azure AD Dashboard>Click Groups in left pane>All Groups Blade opens>In Right pane Click AZ-MZ Group Created in previous exercise>AZ-MZ Group dashboard opens as shown below>Click licenses in left pane> License blade opens as shown below> Note the + Assignments option in right pane.

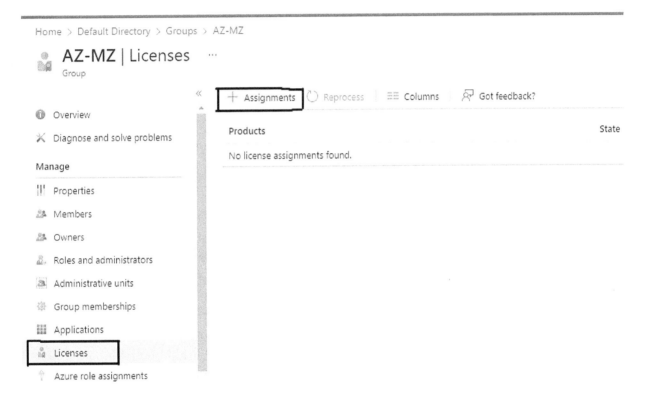

2. In above figure Click + Assignments in right pane>Update License assignments blade opens as shown below> Select Enterprise Mobility + Security E5> Click Save > After you get the notification that License assignments to the member succeeded, Close the Update license assignments blade.

Home > AZ-MZ >

Update license assignments ...

Select licenses

☑ Enterprise Mobility + Security E5

Review license options

| Enterprise Mobility + Security E5 ∨ |

Enterprise Mobility + Security E5

☑ Microsoft Defender for Identity

☑ Microsoft Defender for Cloud Apps

☑ Azure Information Protection Premium P2

☑ Azure Information Protection Premium P1

☑ Azure Rights Management

☑ Microsoft Intune

☑ Azure Active Directory Premium P2

☑ Microsoft Azure Multi-Factor Authentication

☑ Azure Active Directory Premium P1

Save

3. You will be back in AZ-MZ group license blade> Refresh the screen by clicking F5 on your laptop and you can see that the licenses are assigned.

4. Go to User User1 Profile pane and click licenses in left pane> You can see that Enterprise Mobility + Security E5 license is active and the license is inherited from AZ-MZ Group.

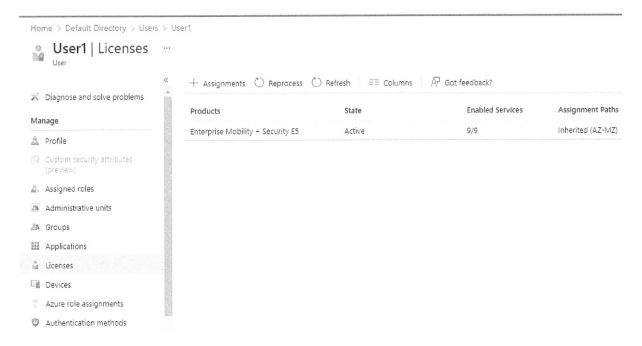

Azure Multi-Factor Authentication

Multifactor Authentication (**MFA**) is a security system that requires more than one method of authentication apart from username/password.

Azure Multifactor Authentication (MFA) provides a second level of security when signing into cloud-based or on-premises applications apart from user password. When enabled, Azure MFA can be configured to verify a user's identity using a call to a mobile or landline phone, a text message, a mobile app notification, Mobile app verification code or 3rd party OATH tokens.

Step by Step Enabling MFA

1. Enable MFA for User.
2. Register User for MFA.

The above steps are interchangeable. You also have the option of registering User for MFA first and then enable MFA for the User.

In case you first enable MFA for the User, the user is then forced to register for MFA when he logs on to Azure Portal.

Very Important Note: When you register Azure AD User for MFA, the User is automatically gets registered for Self Service Password Reset (SSPR) also.

Authentication Options available for MFA

Authentication method	MFA
Microsoft Authenticator app	✓
OATH hardware tokens (preview)	✓
OATH software tokens	✓
SMS	✓
Voice	✓

Exercise 8.13: Enable MFA for Azure AD User User3

In this Exercise we will enable MFA for User2. Azure AD User User3 was created in Exercise 8.4 in this Chapter.

1. In Chrome Browser while logged on with Subscription Administrator credentials, Go to Azure AD Dashboard as shown in Exercise 7.1> Click Users in left pane> All Users blade opens as shown below> Note the **Per-user MFA** option in right pane.

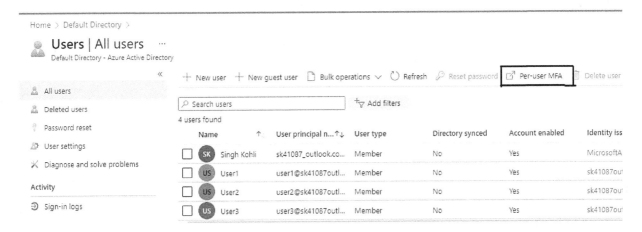

2. Click **Per-user MFA** in above figure> A new Chrome Browser tab opens as shown below> Select User3> Note the Enable option under quick steps.

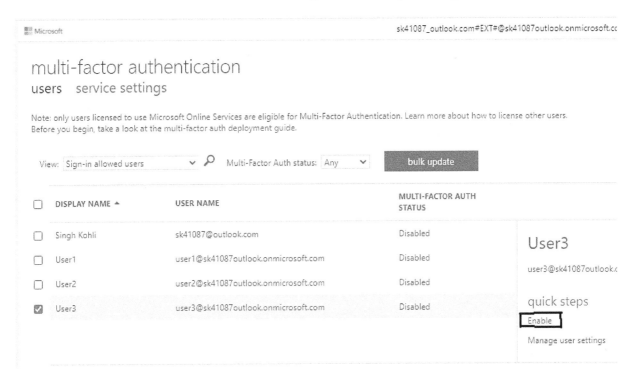

3. In above figure Click Enable under quick steps> A Box pops as shown below> Click enable multi-factor auth>Click Close.

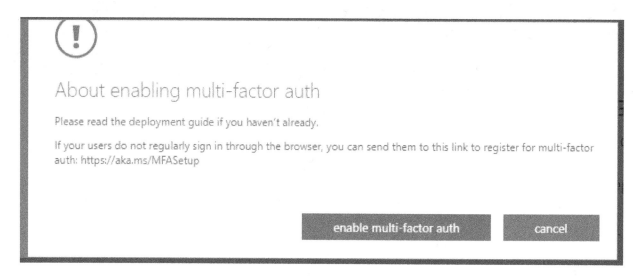

4. Back in Chrome Browser Tab you can see that MFA is enabled for User3.

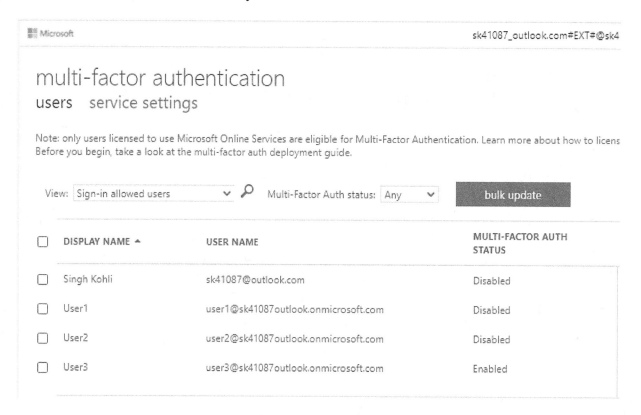

5. Close the Browser Tab for MFA User Settings.

Exercise 8.14: Forced Registration of User3 for MFA using SMS Code

In this exercise User3 will be forced to register for MFA when he logs on to Azure Portal. User3 was created in Exercise 8.4 in this Chapter.

1. Open **Firefox Browser** and go to https://portal azure.com and Log on with User2 Credentials (user3@sk41087outlook.onmicrosoft.com) and Password> Following Pane appears after you enter password. It is asking for more information required.

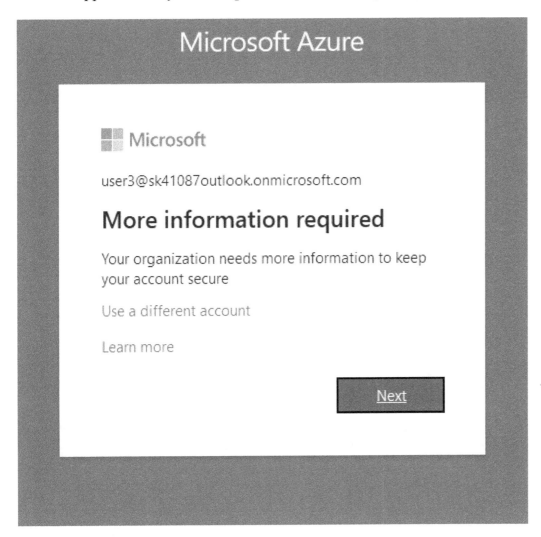

2. Click next in above figure>Keep your account secure pane opens> By default it is giving you Microsoft Authenticator App option for second Authentication. But we want to use Mobile Phone SMS option> Note the link **I want to set up a different method.**

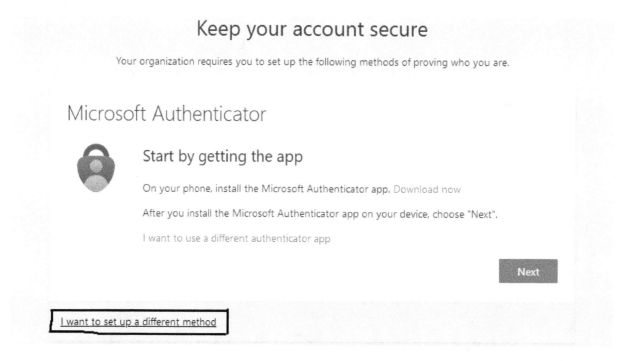

3. In above figure Click the link **I want to set up a different method**>Choose a different Method Box Pops up as shown below> Chose Phone from dropdown box and click Confirm.

4. Keep your account secure pane opens with Phone option>Select your country from dropdown box. In my case I selected India. In Book readers case they need to select their Country>Enter your Mobile Number>Click Next.

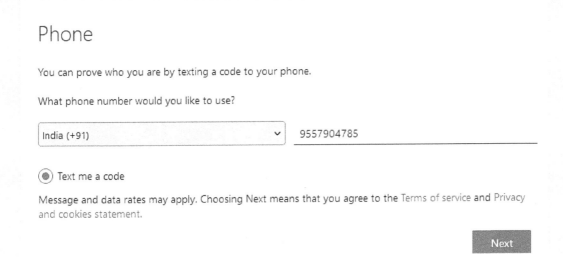

Keep your account secure

Your organization requires you to set up the following methods of proving who you are.

Phone

You can prove who you are by texting a code to your phone.

What phone number would you like to use?

| India (+91) | 9557904785 |

⦿ Text me a code

Message and data rates may apply. Choosing Next means that you agree to the Terms of service and Privacy and cookies statement.

[Next]

5. A new pane opens asking you to enter SMS code sent to your Mobile>Enter the code received on your Mobile and Click Next

Keep your account secure

Your organization requires you to set up the following methods of proving who you are.

Phone

We just sent a 6 digit code to +91 9557904785. Enter the code below.

075944

Resend code

[Back]   [Next]

6. You get notification of Successful verification of SMS>Click Next.

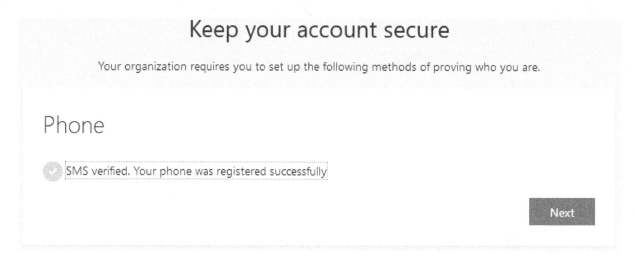

7. You will get notification of Success> Click Done.

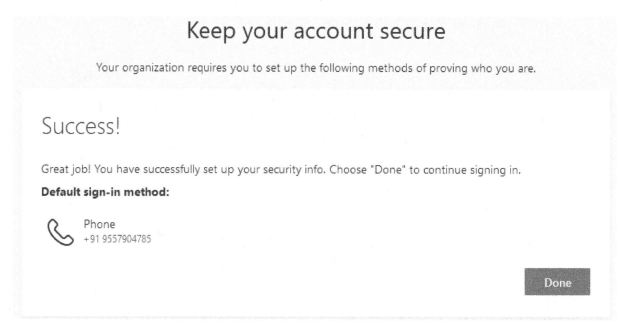

8. In Firefox User3 is now logged on to Azure Portal.
9. In Firefox logout User3 from Azure Portal by clicking Profile icon in Top right and then click Sign out.

Exercise 8.15: Test MFA for Azure AD User User3

1. Open Firefox Browser and enter https://portal.azure.com and Log on with User3 credentials: user3@sk41087outlook.onmicrosoft.com.

2. After you enter the password for User3, following pane will open> In below figure Click on the Row containing your mobile number> Another pane opens asking you to enter code sent to your mobile> Enter Code received on your Mobile and click Verify.

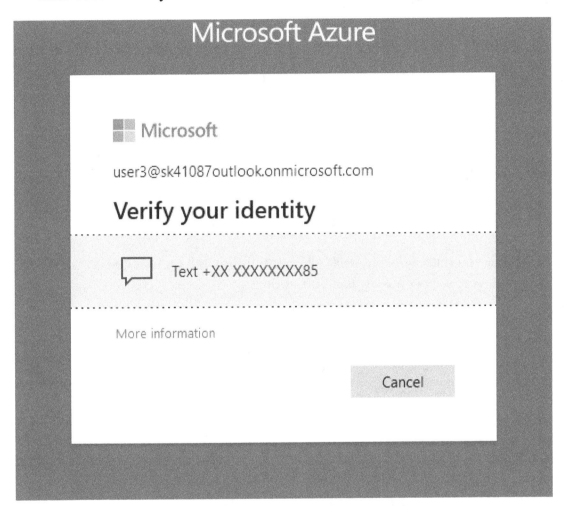

3. In Firefox User3 is now logged on to Azure Portal.
4. In Firefox logout User3 from Azure Portal by clicking Profile icon in Top right and then click Sign out from dropdown box.

Self Service Password Reset (SSPR)

SSPR options allows users to change, reset and unlock there Azure AD login passwords.

SSPR option free's the helpdesk of password service queries and allow them to concentrate on more pressing issues. Helpdesk is an expensive resource. With SSPR option you can reduce the helpdesk cost.

Azure AD license Requirement for SSPC and SSPR

Self-Service Password Reset/Change/Unlock with on-premises <u>writeback</u> for hybrid users: Requires AD Premium P1 or Premium P2 editions.

Number of Authentication methods required

This option determines the minimum number of the available authentication methods a user must go through to reset or unlock their password. **It can be set to either one or two.**

Authentication methods available for Self-Service Password Reset

If SSPR is enabled, you must select at least one of the following options for the authentication methods. You can also select all of them.

Mobile app notification
Mobile app code
Email
Mobile phone
Office phone
Security questions

Step by Step Enabling SSPR

1. Enable SSPR for User.
2. Register User for SSPR/MFA.

The above steps are interchangeable. You also have the option of registering User for SSPR/MFA first and then enable MFA for the User.

In case you first enable SSPR for the User, the user is then forced to register for SSPR/MFA when he logs on to Azure Portal.

Important Note: When you register Azure AD User for MFA, the User is automatically gets registered for Self Service Password Reset (SSPR) also.

Options for enabling Self-Service Password Reset (SSPR) for Azure AD Users

You can either enable SSPR for All Azure AD Users or for Azure AD Groups.

You can't enable SSPR for Specific User or Users unless they are part of Azure AD Group.

Very Important Note: When you register Azure AD User for MFA, the User is automatically gets registered for Self Service Password Reset (SSPR) also.

Exercise 8.16: Create Azure AD Group and Add Azure AD Users

In this lab we will create Azure AD Group **AZ-SSPR** and add Azure AD User User3 to the group manually. Azure AD Users User3 was created in Exercise 8.4.

1. In Azure AD Dashboard Click Groups >All Groups Blade opens>Click + New Group> Add New Group Blade opens as shown below>Select Group type as Security>For Group name enter **AZ-SSPR**> For Azure AD roles can be assigned to the group, select the default **No** option>Select Membership type **Assigned**>Click the Link **No members selected**> Add members pane opens in extreme right> In search pane enter User and select User3 and User3 will now appear under Selected Items> Click Select>Click Create.

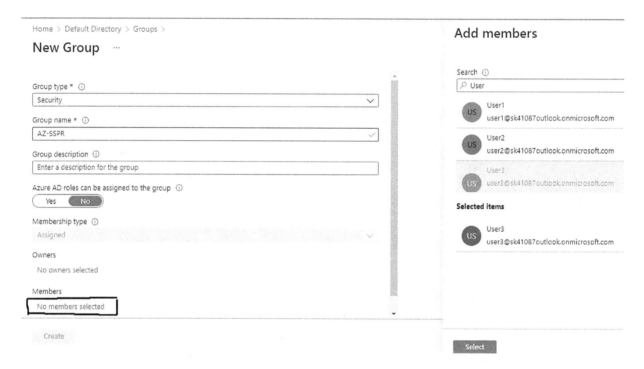

2. Back in All Groups pane you can see the Group AZ-SSPR (2nd Row).

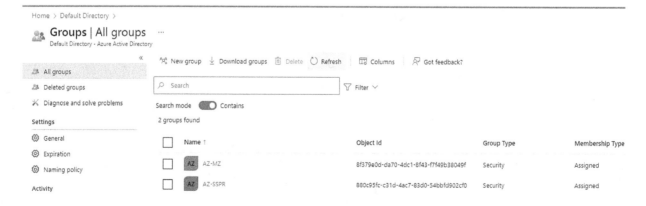

Exercise 8.17: Enabling SSPR for Azure AD Group AZ-SSPR

In this exercise we will enable SSPR for Azure AD Group AZ-SSPR. Azure AD Group AZ-SSPR consists of User3. User3 was created in Exercise 8.4. Azure AD Group AZ-SSPR was created in previous exercise.

1. In Chrome Browser while logged on with Subscription Administrator credentials, Go to Azure AD Dashboard as shown in Exercise 7.1> Azure AD Dashboard opens as shown below> Scroll down in left pane and you can see Password reset option.

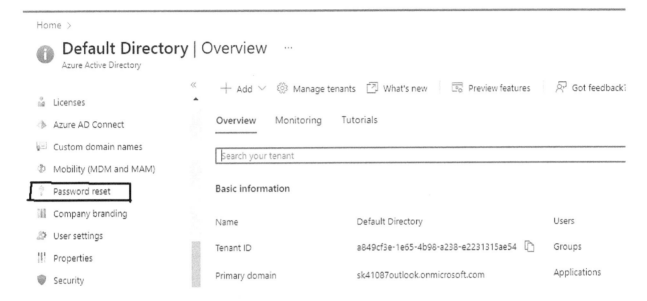

2. In above figure Click Password reset in left pane>Password Reset Blade opens in right pane as shown below> Click **Selected**. Select Group option opens below> Click link No groups selected> Default password reset policy pane opens in extreme right pane>Select Group AZ-SSPR and it will appear under Selected group>Click Select (Not Shown).

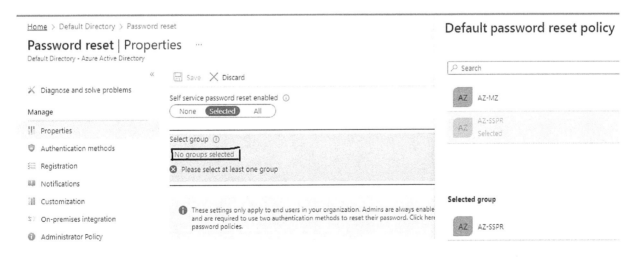

3. Back in Password Reset pane you can see Group AZ-SSPR> **Click Save.**

4. In above figure click Authentication methods in left pane>Select **1** for Number of Methods required for reset> Select **Email** and **Mobile Phone** for Methods available and click **Save.** Since these are default option so Save is not highlighted.
   Note: Readers can choose methods available as per their company Business and Technical requirements.

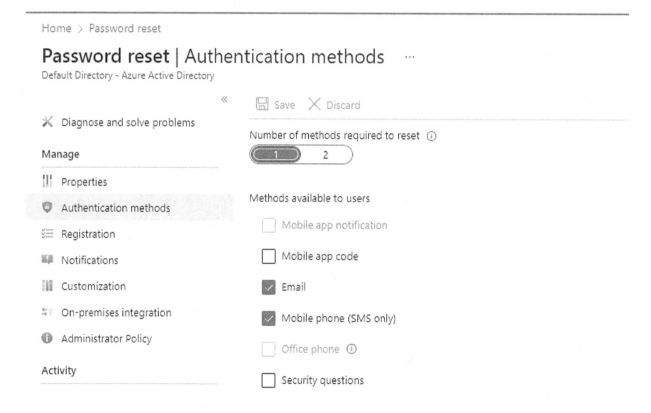

5. <u>After these steps are enabled, then whenever Azure AD User User3 logs on to Azure Portal he will be forced to update contact details for registering for SSPR/MFA. **In our case User3 was already registered for SSPR/MFA using Mobile Phone SMS option in Exercise 8.14**</u>

Exercise 8.18: Test SSPR for Azure AD User User3

In this Exercise we will test Self Service Password Reset (SSPR) for Azure AD User User3. Azure AD User User3 was created in Exercise 7.4. User3 was registered for MFA/SSPR using Mobile Phone SMS option in Exercise 7.14. In previous Exercise we enabled SSPR for Azure AD Group AZ-SSPR. User3 was made member of Azure AD Group AZ-SSPR in Exercise 7.16.

1. Open Firefox and sign-in with User3 credentials: user3@sk41087outlook.onmicrosoft.com> Enter password pane opens as shown below> Note the **Forgot my password** option.

2. In above figure click **Forgot my password** option> Get back into your account pane opens as shown below> enter User3 Sign-in id: (user3@sk41087outlook.onmicrosoft.com) and capcha and click Next.

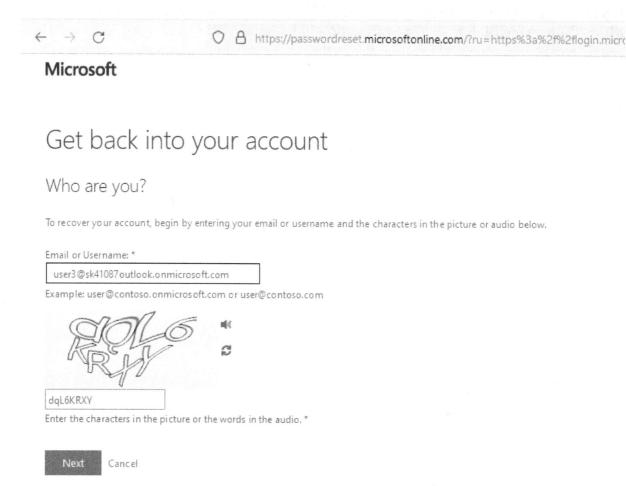

3. Get Back into your account verification pane opens> Enter your mobile number with country code>Click Text. Make sure to add + before country code.

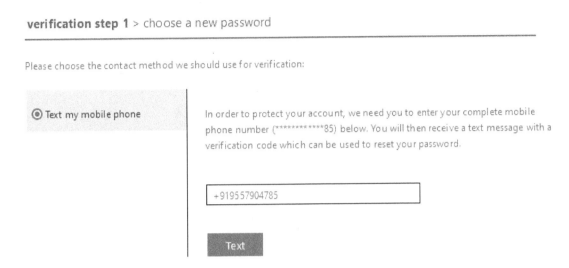

4. Get Back into your account verification pane opens> Enter SMS code received on your mobile>Click Next.

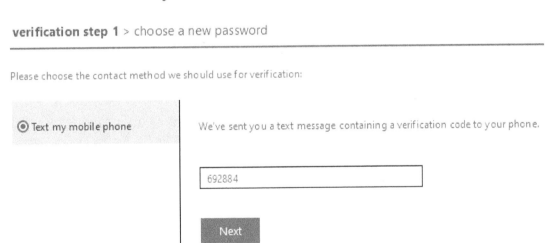

5. Get Back into your account verification pane opens>Enter New Password> Confirm New Password> Click Finish.

Microsoft

Get back into your account

verification step 1 ✓ > **choose a new password**

---

* Enter new password:

```
••••••••••••••
```

strong

* Confirm new password:

```
••••••••••••••
```

Finish   Cancel

6. You get notification that Password has been reset.

← → C   🛡 🔒 https://passwordreset.microsoftonline.com/Done.aspx?ru=

Microsoft

Get back into your account
✓ Your password has been reset

To sign in with your new password, click here.

Chapter 9 Role Based Access Control (RBAC)

Role types

Azure Roles: Azure roles are used to manage access to <u>Azure resources.</u>

Azure AD Roles: Azure AD roles are used to manage access to <u>Azure AD resources.</u>

Comparing Azure roles and Azure AD roles

Azure Roles	Azure AD Roles
Manage access to Azure resources.	Manage access to Azure Active Directory resources.
Supports custom roles.	Supports custom roles.
Scope can be specified at multiple levels (management group, subscription, resource group, resource).	**Scope can be specified at the tenant level (organization-wide), administrative unit, or on an individual object (for example, a specific application).**
Role information can be accessed in Azure portal, Azure CLI, Azure PowerShell, Azure Resource Manager templates, REST API.	Role information can be accessed in Azure portal, Microsoft 365 admin center, Microsoft Graph, AzureAD PowerShell.

Azure Roles

<u>By default Azure AD users have no access to Azure Resources.</u>

For Global Administrator, Limited Administrator & Users to manage or create Azure resources they must be assigned permissions to Azure Roles using Role based Access Control (RBAC).

Azure Roles are used to manage access to Azure resources. Azure role-based access control (Azure RBAC) is used to assign Azure Roles. Azure role-based access control (Azure RBAC) helps you manage who has access to Azure resources, what they can do with those resources, and what areas they have access to.

Built-in high level Azure Roles (Important Concept)

Owner has full access to all resources including the right to delegate access to others.
Contributor can create and manage all types of Azure resources but can't grant access to others.
Reader can view existing Azure resources.

The above Roles apply to all Resource types.

Built-in specific Azure Roles

Azure has Built-in specific Roles which apply to specific Resources only.

Following is a **partial list** of built-in Azure roles available.

RBAC Built in Roles	Description
Backup Contributor	Let's you manage backup service, but you can't create vaults and give access to others.
Backup Reader	Can view backup services, but can't make changes.
Virtual Machine Contributor	Create and manage virtual machines, manage disks and disk snapshots, install and run software, reset password etc. This role does not grant you management access to the virtual network or storage account the virtual machines are connected to.
User Access Administrator	Let's you manage user access to Azure resources.

Azure Role-Based Access Control (RBAC) working

A role assignment is the process of attaching a **role definition** to a **user, group, service principal, or managed identity** at a particular **scope** for the purpose of granting access. Access is granted by creating a role assignment, and access is revoked by removing a role assignment.

A role assignment consists of following three Components:

- Security principal (A security principal is an object that represents a user, group, service principal, or managed identity).
- Role definition or Role.
- Scope.

Scope

Scope is the level at which Roles are applied. You can specify a scope at four levels: Management group, Subscription, Resource group or Resource.

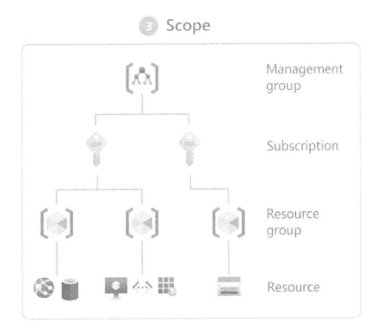

How RBAC Permissions are assigned

RBAC permissions are assigned using **Access Control (IAM) Tab** in Resource or Resource Group, Subscription or Management Group Dashboard.

Exercise 9.1: Check Built-in Azure Roles available

You can check Built-in Azure Roles available by clicking Access Control (IAM) option in left pane in Management Group, Subscription, Resource Group or Resource Dashboard. In this Exercise we will check Built-in Azure Roles available at Subscription level.

1. Open Chrome Browser and go to Azure Portal @ portal.azure.com using Subscription Administrator credentials and password> Azure Portal opens as shown below. In Azure Portal Click 3 Horizontal lines in top left> A pane opens in left of Azure Portal> Note the **All services** option in left pane.

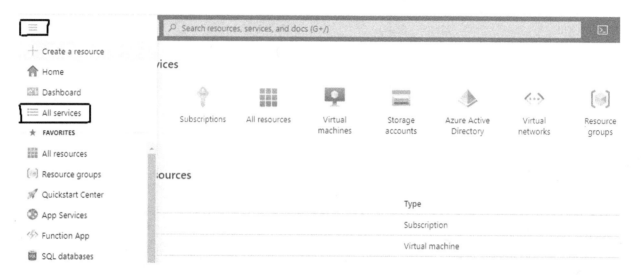

2. In Azure Portal Click All services in left pane> In All Services pane opens as shown below> In All services pane click General in left pane> In right pane note the Subscription option.

3. In above figure click Subscriptions in right pane>All Subscription pane opens as shown below. Note the Subscription with name Free Trial.

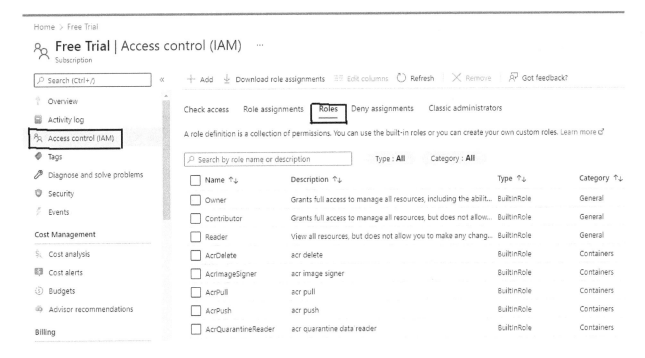

4. In above figure Click Your Subscription> Subscription Dashboard opens as shown below> Click Access control (IAM) option in left pane> In right pane click Roles> Roles pane opens as shown below. You can see all the Built-in Azure Roles available. Readers are requested to scroll down and see all the Azure Roles available.

5. As an Exercise to readers check Azure Roles available at Resource level. Use Resource Virtual Machine vmcloud1. Virtual Machine vmcloud1 was created in Exercise 6.1 in Chapter 6. Compare Number of Azure Roles available in VM vmcloud1 with Step 4 Azure Roles available at Subscription level.

Exercise 9.2: Check Azure AD User User1 Access to Azure Resources

In this exercise we will check Azure AD User User1 Access to Azure Resources. User1 was created in Exercise 8.2 in Chapter 8 with Directory role of Global Administrator.

1. Open **Firefox** and Log on to Azure portal @ https://portal.azure.com with User1 Credentials (**user1@sk41087outlook.onmicrosoft.com**) and password. You can see there are no resources to display for User1 and user has no access to resources and User cannot create any resources.
   I tried to create Azure VM but was not able to create it.

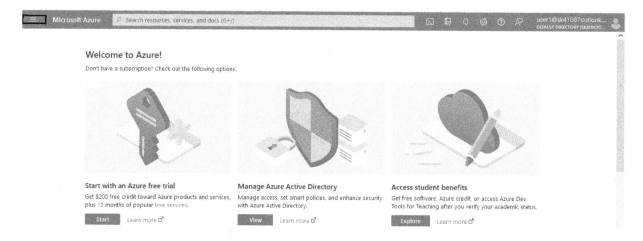

2. In above figure Click 3 Horizontal lines in top left> A pane opens in left of Azure Portal as shown below> Note the All resources option in left pane.

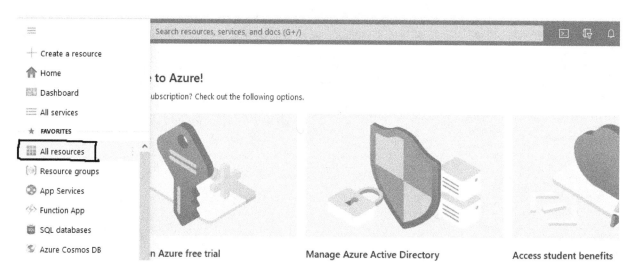

3. In above figure Click All resources in left pane and you can see there are no Azure resources to display.

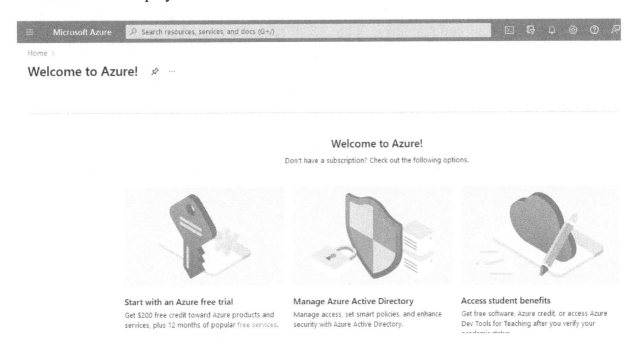

4. **<u>Azure AD Users access to Azure resource requires Role based Access control (RBAC).</u>** In next exercise using RBAC we will assign User1 role of Contributor at Subscription level.

5. In Firefox logout User1 from Azure Portal.

Exercise 9.3: Assign Contributor Role to User1 at Subscription level

In this exercise we will assign User1 role of Contributor at Subscription level. With Contributor role User1 can manage and create all resources in subscription but cannot delegate access to other users. User1 was created in Exercise 8.2 in Chapter 8.

1. Open Chrome Browser and go to Azure Portal @ portal.azure.com using Subscription Administrator credentials and password> In Azure Portal Click 3 Horizontal lines in top left> A pane opens in left of Azure Portal> In Azure Portal Click All services in left pane> In All services pane click General> In right pane click Subscriptions>All Subscription pane opens>Click Your Free Trial Subscription> Subscription Dashboard opens as shown below> Note the Access control (IAM) option in left pane.

2. In Subscription Dashboard click Access Control (IAM) in left pane> Access Control pane opens as shown below> Note the Add role assignment option in right pane.

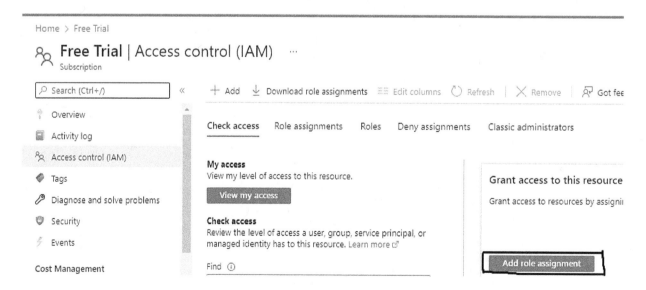

3. In above figure click Add role assignment. Add role assignment blade with Role option opens as shown below> Select the Row containing Built-in role Contributor > Note the Next option.

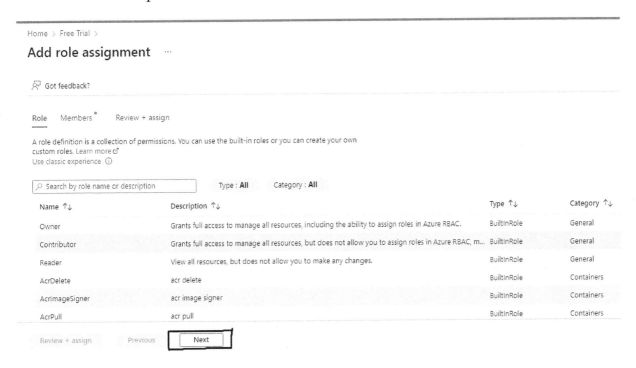

4. In above figure click Next> Add role assignment blade with Members option opens as shown below> Note the + Select members option.

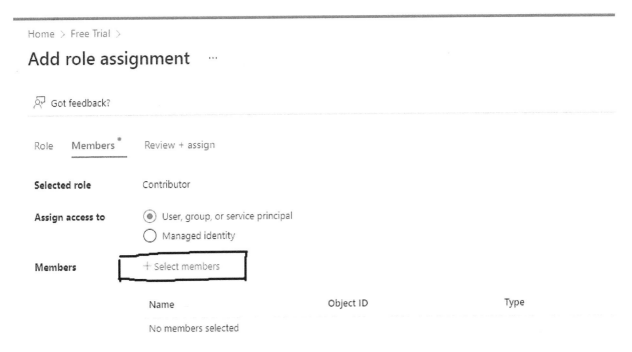

5. In above figure click + Select members> Select members pane opens a shown below> Select Azure AD User User1 and it will appear under Selected members.

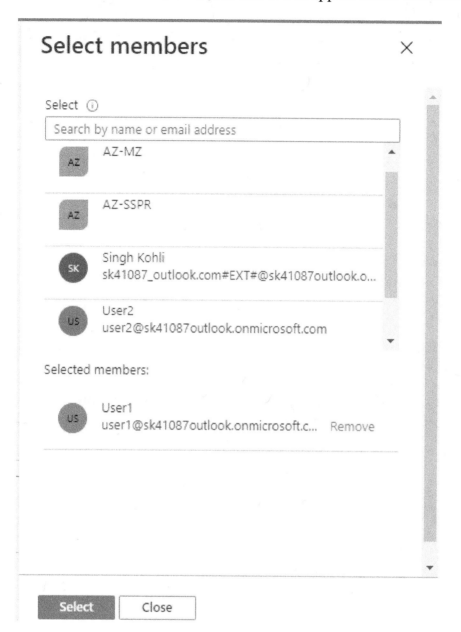

6. In above figure Click Select and you will be back in Add role assignment blade with Members option as shown below. Note that User1 now appears under Members.

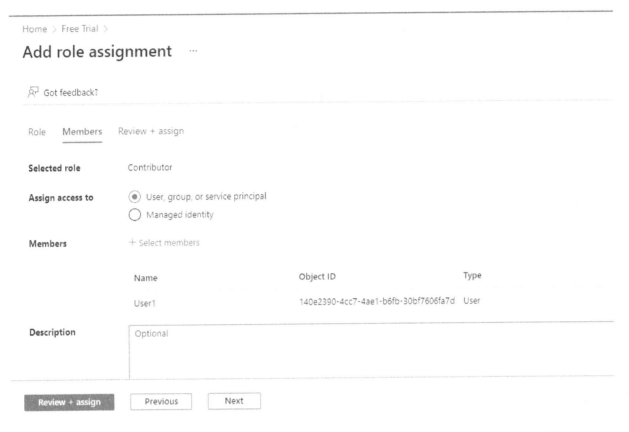

7. In above figure Click Next> Review + assign pane opens as shown below> Click Review + assign.

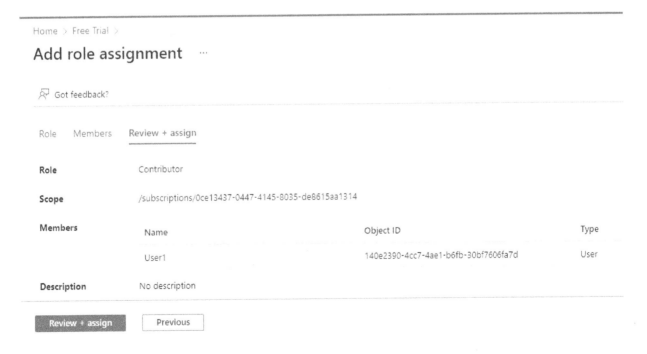

8. You will be back In Access Control pane> Click Role assignments in right pane> As shown below Azure AD User User1 is now assigned the role of Contributor at Subscription level.

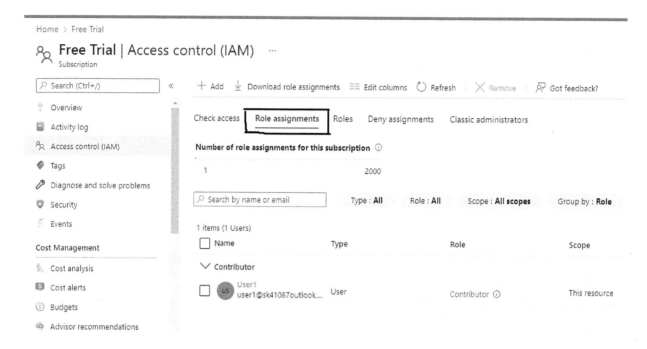

Exercise 9.4: Check Azure AD User User1 Access to Azure Resources again

1. Open **Firefox** and Log on to Azure Portal @ https://portal.azure.com with User1 credentials: user1@sk41087outlook.onmicrosoft.com.
2. In Azure Portal Click 3 Horizontal lines in top left> A pane opens in left of Azure Portal> Click All resources in left pane> All Resources Panes opens as shown below> You can see all the Azure Resources which we have created till now. Scroll down to see more Azure resources.

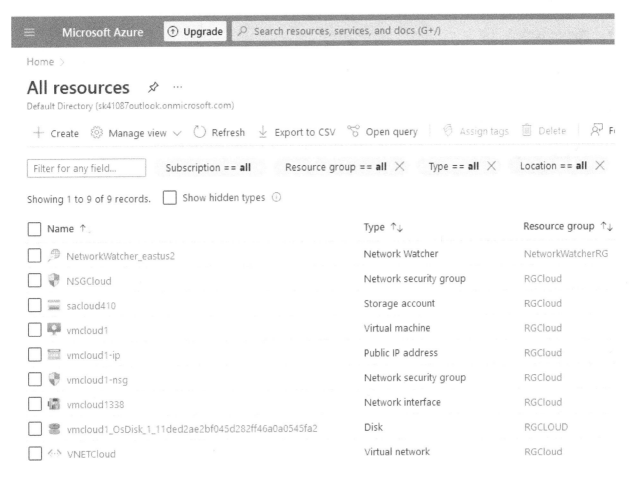

3. As an Exercise to readers try to create Storage Account and it will succeed. See Exercise 7.1 in Chapter 7 on how to create Storage Account.

4. In Firefox Logout User1 from Azure portal by clicking Profile icon in top right and then clicking sign out.

Chapter 10 Azure Security

In Azure Cloud you get multiple options to protect Azure Resources.

- Network Security Groups
- Application Security Groups
- Azure Firewall
- Web Application Firewall
- Azure Bastion Host
- Azure Key Vault

Additionally you can restrict Access to Azure Resources using following options:

- Resource Firewall
- Service Endpoints
- Private Endpoints
- Role Based Access Control (RBAC)

In this Chapter we will focus on Network Security Groups only.

We have already discussed Role Based Access Control (RBAC) option in previous Chapter.

Network Security Groups

Network Security Group (NSG) is Virtual Firewall. NSGs control **inbound** and **outbound** access to network interfaces (NICs) and subnets. Each NSG contains one or more rules specifying whether or not traffic is approved or denied based on source IP address, source port, destination IP address, destination port and protocol.

NSGs can be associated with subnets and network interfaces of Virtual Machines within that subnet. When a NSG is associated with a subnet, the ACL rules apply to all the VM instances in that subnet. In addition, traffic to an individual VM can be further restricted by associating a NSG directly to that VM NIC.

Figure below Shows VNET with 2 Subnets. Virtual Machine in Web-Subnet is protected by 2 Levels of NSG – NSG at Subnet level and NSG at Virtual Machine Network Interface level. Whereas Virtual Machine in DB-Subnet is protected by one level of NSG applied at Virtual Machine Network Interface Level.

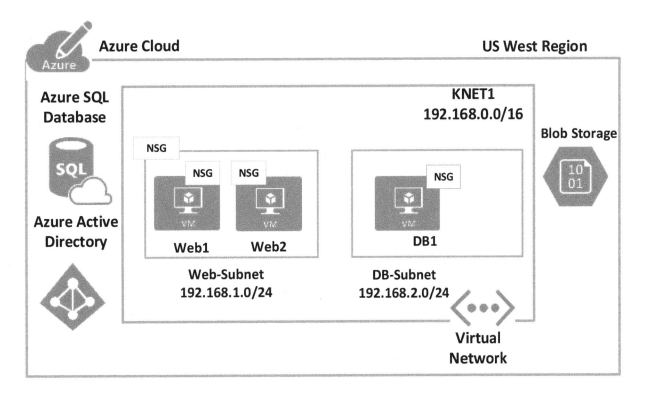

Default NSG Rules

NSGs contain a set of default rules. The default rules cannot be deleted. <u>Default rules can be overridden by creating new rules with higher priority.</u> **Higher the Number Lower the priority.**

Default Inbound rules

Name	Priority	Source IP	Src Port	Dest IP	Dest Port	Protocol	Access
ALLOW VNET INBOUND	65000	VIRTUAL NETWORK	*	VIRTUAL NETWORK	*	*	Allow
ALLOW AZURE LOAD BALANCER INBOUND	65001	AZURE LOADBALANCER	*	*	*	*	Allow
DENY ALL INBOUND	65500	*	*	*	*	*	Deny

Default Outbound rules

Name	Priority	Source IP	Src Port	Dest IP	Dest Port	Protocol	Access
ALLOW VNET OUTBOUND	65000	VIRTUAL NETWORK	*	VIRTUAL NETWORK	*	*	Allow
ALLOW INTERNET OUTBOUND	65001	*	*	Internet	*	*	Allow
DENY ALL OUTBOUND	65500	*	*	*	*	*	Deny

- * Represent all addresses, Ports & Protocols.

We can infer following from the above default rules:

1. All VM to VM traffic within subnet or between subnets is allowed.
2. VM to internet traffic is allowed.
3. Azure Load balancer to VM is allowed.
4. Inbound internet to VM is blocked.
5. <u>Default rules can be overridden by creating new rules with higher priority.</u> **Higher the Number Lower the priority or Lower the Number Higher the Priority.**

Effective NSG Permissions

NSG can be applied at Subnet or VM NIC level or both at Subnet and VM NIC Level.

Let's take an example to check what's the effective traffic reaching Virtual Machine when NSG is applied at both Subnet and VM NIC level. We have 2 VMs (App-Prod & App-Test) created in App Subnet as shown in below figure.

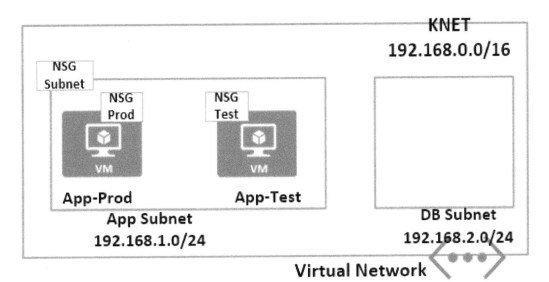

NSGSubnet has 3 inbound allow rules - http, https & RDP.
NSGProd has 2 inbound allow rules - https & RDP.
NSGTest has 2 inbound allow rules - http & RDP.

Effective traffic entering the subnet is http, https & RDP. NSGSubnet blocks any other traffic apart from http, https & RDP.

Effective traffic entering VM App-prod is https & RDP. NSGProd blocks http traffic.

Effective traffic entering VM App-Test is http & RDP. NSGTest blocks https traffic.

Exercise 10.1: Create Network Security Group (NSG) with default rules

In this Exercise we will create Network Security Group with name **NSGCloud** in resource group **RGCloud** and in **US East 2** Location with default rules. Resource group RGCloud was created in Exercise 4.1 in Chapter 4.

1. Open Chrome Browser and log on to Azure Portal @ portal.azure.com using Subscription Administrator credentials and password> Azure Portal opens as shown below. In Azure Portal Click 3 Horizontal lines in top left> A pane opens in left of Azure Portal> Note the **All services** option in left pane.

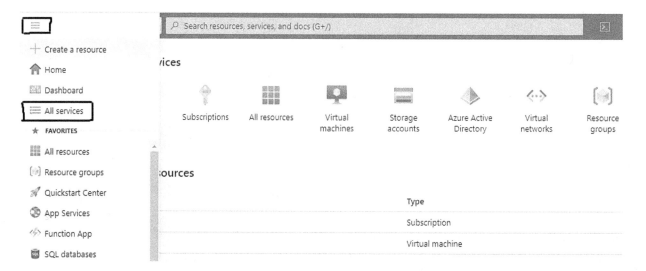

2. In Azure Portal Click All services in left pane> In All Services pane opens as shown below> In All services pane click Networking in left pane> In right pane note the Network security groups (NSG) option.

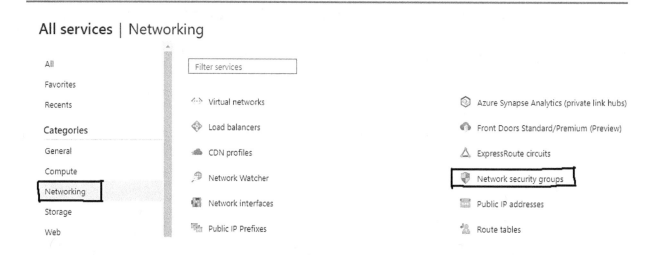

3. In above figure click Network security groups> All Network security groups pane opens as shown below> Note the + Create option.

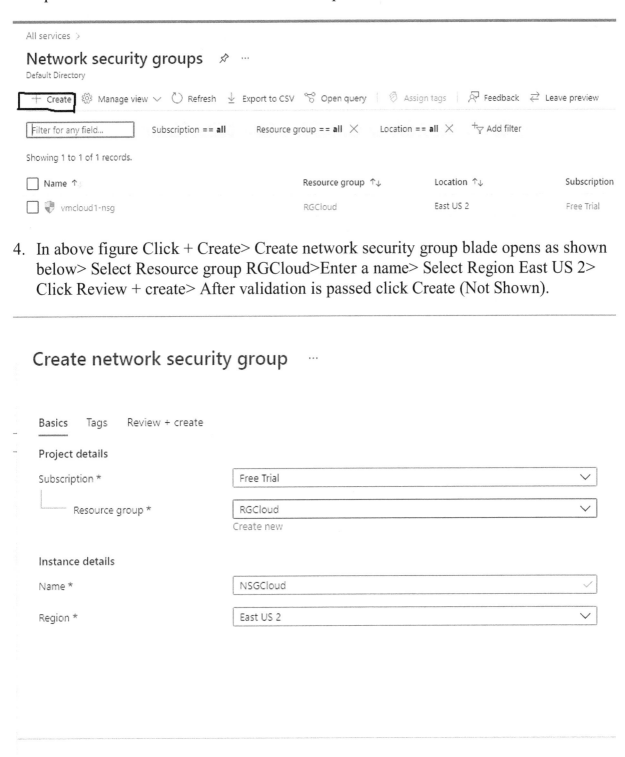

4. In above figure Click + Create> Create network security group blade opens as shown below> Select Resource group RGCloud>Enter a name> Select Region East US 2> Click Review + create> After validation is passed click Create (Not Shown).

5. Figure below shows Network Security Group NSGCloud Dashboard with default inbound and outbound security rules> Note the Subnets option in left pane. We will use this option in next exercise to associate Network Security Group (NSG) NSGCloud with Subnet Web-Subnet> Note the Inbound security rules option in left pane. We will use this option in Exercise 9.4 to add inbound RDP, http & https allow rule.

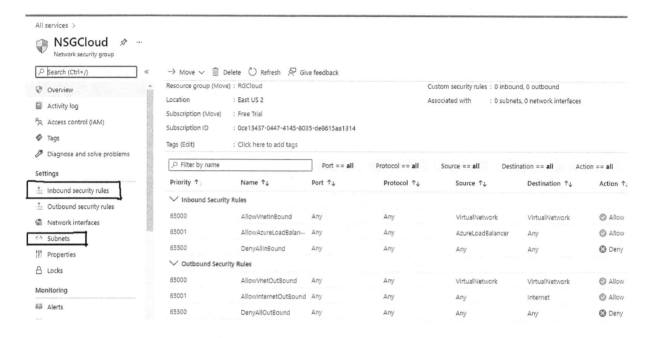

Note on Default Inbound Rules

Note 1: In inbound security rules, all inbound traffic is set to deny (Rule number 3) except for VNET to VNET and Azure Load Balancer to Any.
Note 2: Best Practice is to create a new inbound rule and allow traffic which is needed. Do not make this rule allow for all the traffic.
Note 3: Override Default inbound rule by creating new rule with higher priority or lower number than the default inbound rule.
Note 4: You cannot edit or delete the default rules (65000, 65001 & 65500).

Note on Outbound Rules

Note 1: Internet outbound is allowed.
Note 2: Outbound VNET to VNET is allowed.

Exercise 10.2: Associate Network Security Group (NSG) with Subnet

In this exercise we will associate Network Security Group NSGCloud created in previous exercise with Subnet Web-Subnet in Virtual Network VNETCloud. Virtual Network VNETCloud and Web-Subnet were created in Exercise 5.1 in Chapter 5.

1. In Network Security Group NSGCloud Dashboard click Subnets in left pane> Note the + Associate option in right pane.

2. In above figure click +Associate in right pane> Associate Subnet blade opens as shown below> In Associate Subnet Blade select VNETCloud in Virtual Network & select Web-Subnet in Subnet and click OK (Not Shown).

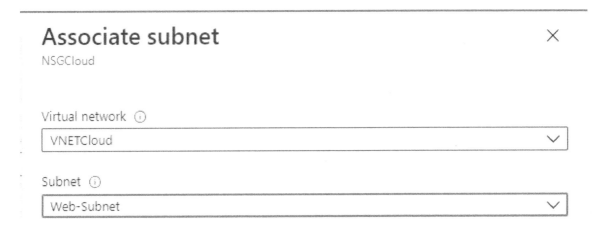

3. Figure below shows that Network Security Group NSGCloud is now associated with Subnet Web-Subnet.

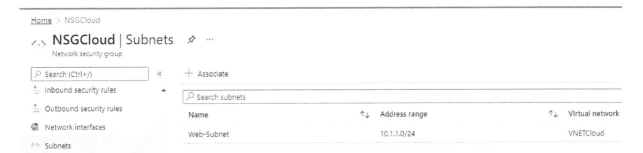

Exercise 10.3: Access Default Website and RDP on Virtual Machine vmfe1

In this Exercise we will check whether we can access default website on Virtual Machine vmcloud1. We will also check whether we can RDP to vmcloud1. Windows VM vmcloud1 was created in Exercise 6.1 in Chapter 6.

1. Go to VM vmcloud1 dashboard. Make sure that vmcloud1 is running. If not then click start. Copy the DNS name of vmcloud1. In my case DNS Address is **vmcloud1.eastus2.cloudapp.azure.com.**
2. Open browser and enter **vmcloud1.eastus2.cloudapp.azure.com**> you can see from below figure you cannot access default website on vmcloud1.

This site can't be reached

vmcloud1.eastus2.cloudapp.azure.com took too long to respond.

Try:

- Checking the connection
- Checking the proxy and the firewall
- Running Windows Network Diagnostics

ERR_CONNECTION_TIMED_OUT

3. When I tried to RDP to VM vmcloud1 it failed.
4. **The reason of above denial of access is that Network Security Group NSGCloud associated with Web-Subnet stopped the inbound http and RDP traffic. Note that Network Security Group NSGCloud only had default rules which prevented inbound http and RDP traffic to Virtual Machine vmfe1.**
5. <u>In next exercise we will add inbound allow rule for RDP, http & https traffic to Network Security Group NSGCloud associated with Web-Subnet.</u>

Exercise 10.4: Add inbound RDP, http and https allow rule in NSG

In this lab we will add inbound RDP, http & https allow rule in Network Security Group NSGCloud created in Exercise 10.1.

1. **Add inbound RDP allow rule**: In NSGCloud dashboard click Inbound security rules in left pane>In Right pane click +Add>Add inbound security rule blade opens as shown below> In Service select **RDP**> In Action select **Allow**> Enter Priority **100**> Give a name to the rule>Rest select all default values> Click Add.

Note: Readers are advised to click the Source and destination drop boxes to see the options.

2. **Add inbound allow http rule**: In NSG dashboard click inbound security rules in left pane>In Right pane click +Add>Add inbound security rule blade opens as shown below> In Service select **HTTP**> In Action select **Allow**> Enter Priority **110**> Give a name to the rule>Rest select all default values> Click Add.

3. **Add inbound allow https rule**: In NSG dashboard click inbound security rules in left pane>In Right pane click +Add>Add inbound security rule blade opens as shown below> In Service select **HTTPS**> In Action select **Allow**> Enter Priority **120**> Give a name to the rule>Rest select all default values> Click Add.

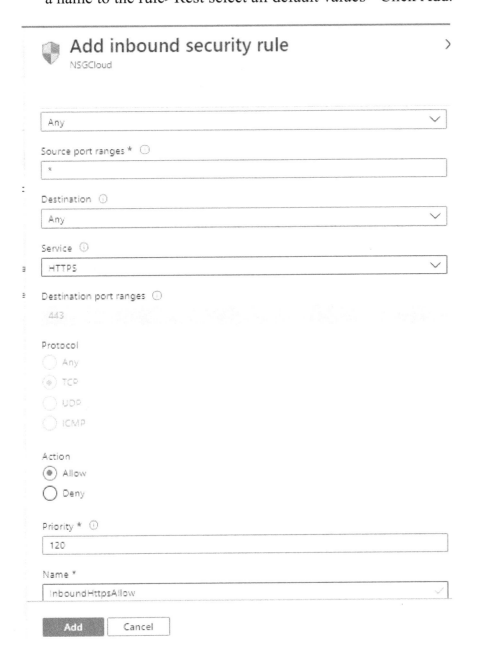

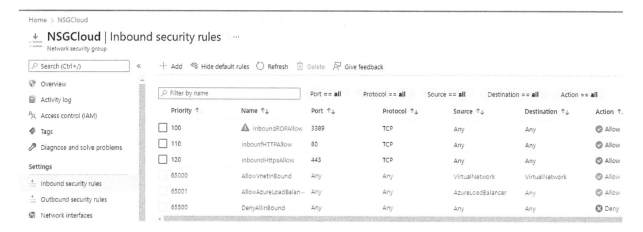

4. Figure below shows inbound security rules pane with 3 new rules added.

Note 1: You can edit the rule by clicking the rule in the right pane or delete the rule by clicking ellipsis …

Note 2: You cannot edit or delete the default rules (65000, 65001 & 65500).

Exercise 10.5: Access Default Website and RDP on Virtual Machine vmcloud1

In this Exercise we will check whether we can access default website on Virtual Machine vmcloud1. We will also check whether we can RDP to Virtual Machine vmcloud1. Windows VM vmcloud1 was created in Exercise 5.1 in Chapter 5.

1. Go to vmfe1 dashboard. Make sure that vmfe1 is running. If not then click start. Copy the DNS name of vmcloud1. In my case DNS Address is **vmcloud1.eastus2.cloudapp.azure.com.**

2. Open browser and enter **vmcloud1.eastus2.cloudapp.azure.com**> You can see that default website on VM vmcloud1 opens as shown below.

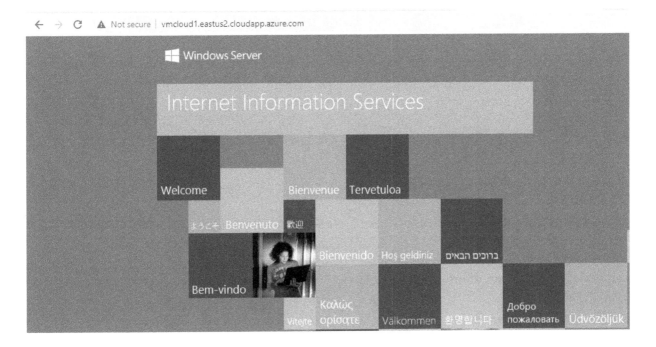

3. RDP to vmcloud1> It was successful.

4. We were able to successfully http and RDP to VM vmcloud1. The reason of this success was that we allowed inbound http and RDP traffic in Network Security Group NSGCloud associated with Subnet Web-Subnet. VM vmcloud1 was created in with Subnet Web-Subnet. NSG on VM vmcloud1 Network interface has 3 inbound allow rules- http, https and RDP. This was configured in step 3 when we created VM vmcloud1 in Exercise 5.1 in Chapter 5.

5. Stop VM vmcloud1.

Chapter 11 Azure SQL Database

Azure SQL Database is a relational database-as-a-service (DBaaS) in the cloud built on the Microsoft SQL Server platform. Azure SQL Database is a managed resource which means we don't have to install, upgrade or patch the database. You also don't have to manage the underlying infrastructure – Hardware and Operating System.

Azure SQL Database Deployment Options

You can Deploy Azure SQL Database in 3 ways as shown in figure below.

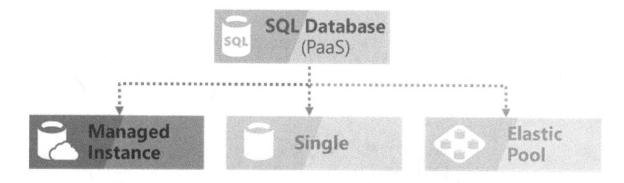

Single Database model creates a Single Database in Azure SQL Database with its own set of resources managed via a single SQL Database server.

An **elastic pool** is a **collection** of databases that have varying and unpredictable usage demands. The databases in an elastic pool are on a single server and share a set number of resources at a set price.

Azure SQL Managed Instance is deployed in Virtual Network. Azure SQL Managed Instance has near 100% compatibility with the latest SQL Server (Enterprise Edition) database engine. Azure SQL Managed Instance database service combines the broadest SQL Server database engine compatibility with all the benefits of a fully managed platform as a service (PaaS).

Azure SQL Database Authentication

SQL Database supports two types of authentication – SQL Authentication and Azure Active Directory Authentication.

SQL Authentication uses a username and password which were specified during database creation.

Azure Active Directory Authentication uses identities managed by Azure Active Directory.

Exercise 11.1: Create Azure SQL Database

In this exercise we will create **Azure SQL Database (Single Database Model)** in **East US 2 Location** and in **Resource Group RGCloud.** Resource Group RGCloud was created in Exercise 4.1 in Chapter 4.

1. Open Chrome Browser and log on to Azure Portal @ portal.azure.com using Subscription Administrator credentials and password> Azure Portal opens as shown below. In Azure Portal Click 3 Horizontal lines in top left> A pane opens in left of Azure Portal as shown below> Note the **All services** option in left pane.

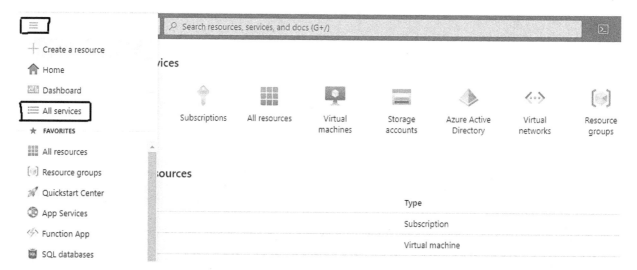

2. In Azure Portal Click All services in left pane> All Services pane opens as shown below> In All services pane click Databases in left pane> In right pane note the SQL databases option.

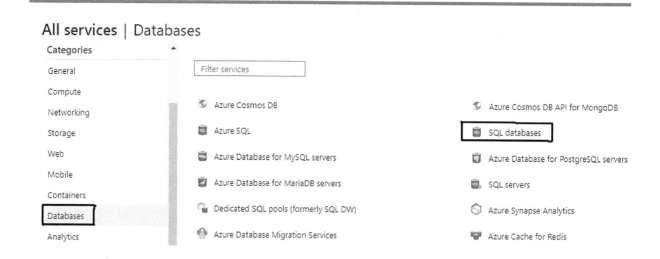

3. In above figure click SQL databases>All SQL Database Pane opens as shown below> Note the + Create option.

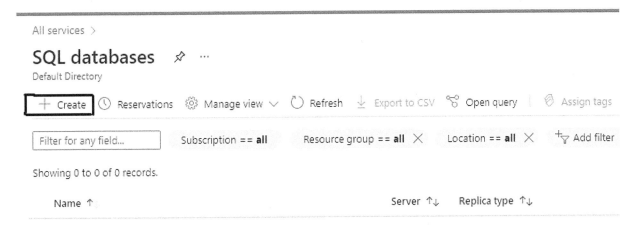

4. In above figure Click + Create> Create SQL Database blade opens as shown below> In Resource Group select RGCloud> Enter a database name. I entered **sqlcloud**> In Server option note the link Create new.

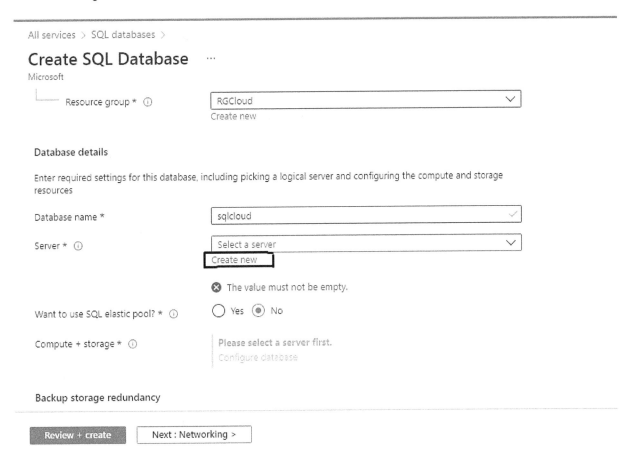

5. In above figure click link Create new> Create SQL Database Server blade opens as shown below> Enter server name. I entered **sqlsrvcloud**> In Location Select East US 2> In Authentication method make sure default option Use SQL Authentication is selected> Enter Server Admin name. I entered **AdminAccount**> Enter password>Confirm Password> Click OK.

All services > SQL databases > Create SQL Database >

Create SQL Database Server ...
Microsoft

Server name *	sqlsrvcloud
	.database.windows.net
Location *	(US) East US 2

Authentication

Select your preferred authentication methods for accessing this server. Create a server admin login and password to access your server with SQL authentication, select only Azure AD authentication Learn more ☑ using an existing Azure AD user, group, or application as Azure AD admin Learn more ☑ , or select both SQL and Azure AD authentication.

Authentication method	⦿ Use SQL authentication
	◯ Use only Azure Active Directory (Azure AD) authentication
	◯ Use both SQL and Azure AD authentication
Server admin login *	AdminAccount
Password *	••••••••••••
Confirm password *	••••••••••••

OK

6. You will be back Create SQL Database Blade> In Want to use SQL Elastic Pool option select **No**> Note the option Configure database.

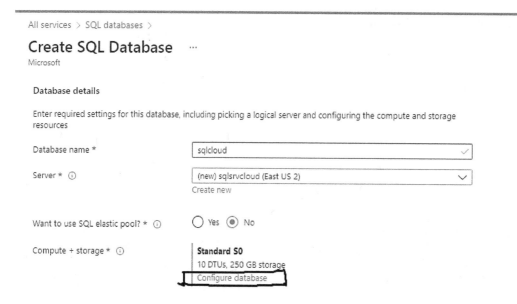

Azure Study & Lab Guide For Beginners

7. In above figure, In Compute + Storage option click link Configure database>
   Configure Database blade opens as shown below> In Service Tier dropdown box
   select **Standard**> Select Default options for DTU & Storage>Click Apply.

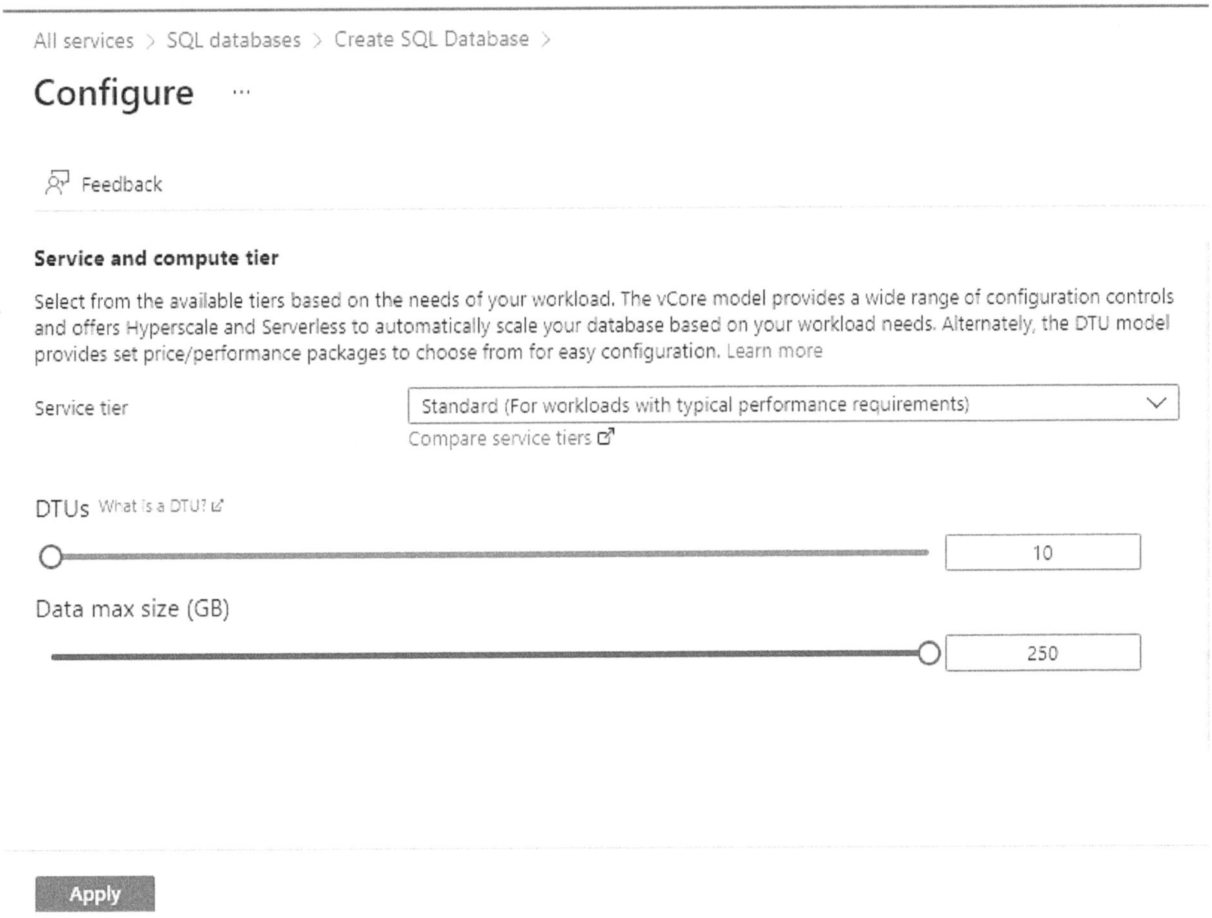

All services > SQL databases > Create SQL Database >

Configure   ⋯

👤 Feedback

Service and compute tier

Select from the available tiers based on the needs of your workload. The vCore model provides a wide range of configuration controls
and offers Hyperscale and Serverless to automatically scale your database based on your workload needs. Alternately, the DTU model
provides set price/performance packages to choose from for easy configuration. Learn more

Service tier
| Standard (For workloads with typical performance requirements) | ⌄ |

Compare service tiers ⧉

DTUs What is a DTU? ⧉

◯── | 10 |

Data max size (GB)

──◯ | 250 |

Apply

8. You will be back in Create SQL Database blade with all options entered> System has automatically selected Geo-redundant backup storage.

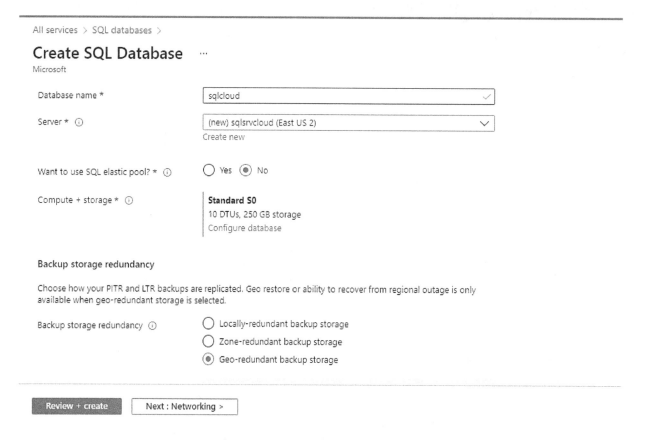

9. In above figure Click Next: Networking>Networking pane opens as shown below> In Network connectivity select Public endpoint> In Firewall Rules select Yes for both the options>Rest select all default values.

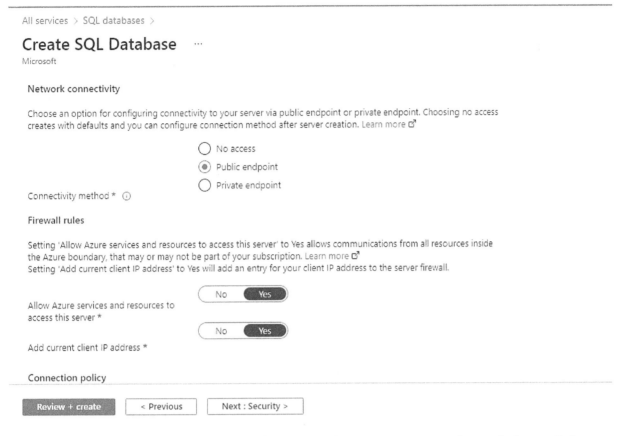

10. In above figure Click Next: Security> Security pane opens as shown below> Select all default values in Security Pane> Click Next: Additional Settings (Not Shown).

All services > SQL databases >

Create SQL Database ···

Microsoft

Basics   Networking   **Security**   Additional settings   Tags   Review + create

Microsoft Defender for SQL

Protect your data using Microsoft Defender for SQL, a unified security package including vulnerability assessment and advanced threat protection for your server. Learn more ⬀

Get started with a 30 day free trial period, and then 1080.6789 INR/server/month.

Enable Microsoft Defender for SQL * ⓘ   ◯ Start free trial
                                          ⦿ Not now

11. Additional Settings pane opens as shown below>Select Sample Tab. This will create AdventureWorksLT as Sample Database.

12. Click Review + Create in above figure> Review + create screen opens as shown below> Click Create (Not Shown). Readers are requested to scroll down this pane and read all the information.

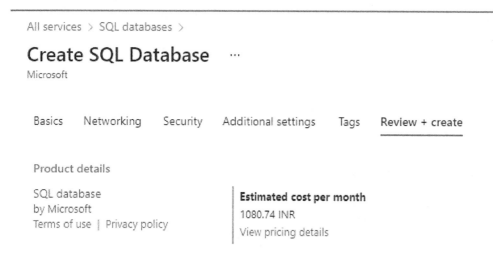

13. Figure below shows dashboard of Azure SQL Database sqlcloud. Note the Server name in right pane. We will use this in SQL Server Management Studio to connect to the Database in next Exercise. In my case Server name is **sqlsrvcloud.database.windows.net.**

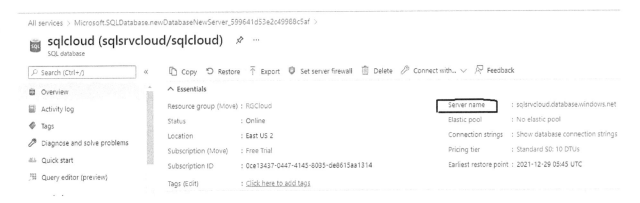

14. In SQL Database sqlcloud Dashboard Click Link in Server name row in right pane>SQL database Server sqlsrv410cloud dashboard opens as shown below.

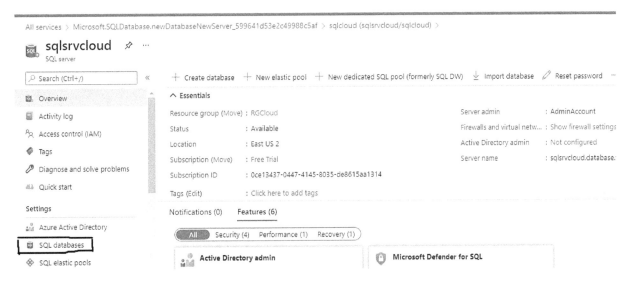

15. To go back to Azure SQL Database sqlcloud dashboard click SQL databases in left pane in above figure> In Right pane click Azure SQL Database sqlcloud> Sql Database sql4cloud dashboard opens.

Important Note: In Azure SQL Database labs we have to work with 2 Dashboards. One for SQL Database sqlcloud Dashboard and one for SQL Database Server sqlsrvcloud Dashboard.

Exercise 11.2: Connect to Azure SQL Database Server sqlsrvcloud

In this Exercise we will connect to Azure SQL Database Server sqlsrvcloud using SQL Server Management Studio (SSMS). Azure SQL Database Server sqlsrvcloud was created in Previous Exercise. In my case DNS name of Azure SQL Database Server sqlsrvcloud is **sqlsrvcloud.database.windows.net.**

For this Lab download and Install SQL Server Management Studio (SSMS) on your laptop from following link. You can also do a Google search for SQL Server Management Studio (SSMS). It will be used in step 3. https://docs.microsoft.com/en-us/sql/ssms/download-sql-server-management-studio-ssms?view=sql-server-ver15 or do a Google search for Download SSMS.

1. On the client machine whose IP was entered in step 9 in previous exercise, open SSMS and enter Azure SQL database server name. In my case it was **sqlsrvcloud.database.windows.net**> In Authentication Select SQL Server Authentication and enter username and password you entered during Azure SQL Database creation time> Click Connect.

2. In SSMS pane Expand Databases> You can see sqlcloud database created in previous exercise> I also expanded Database sqlcloud> I also expanded Tables. You can see that AdventureworksLT sample data has been added to SQL Database sqlcloud. This option was selected in Step 11 in previous exercise.

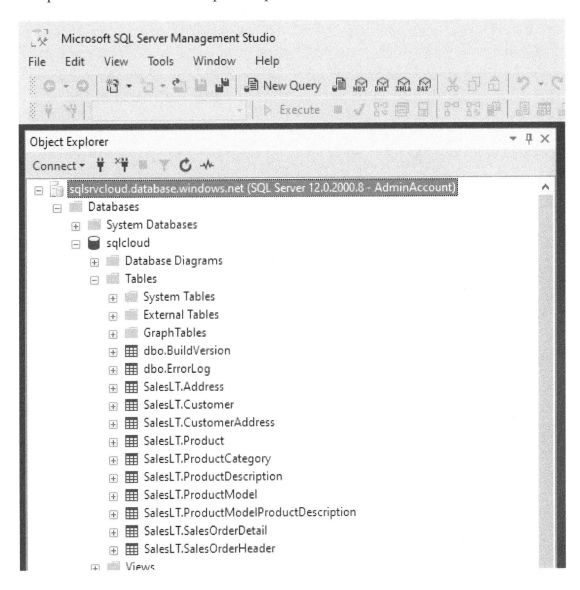

3. Close SSMS

4. **Connection Strings:** For your application to access SQL database you need to add connection strings in the application code. In SQL Database sqlcloud dashboard click **Connection strings** in left pane>In Right pane you can see connection strings for your application type.

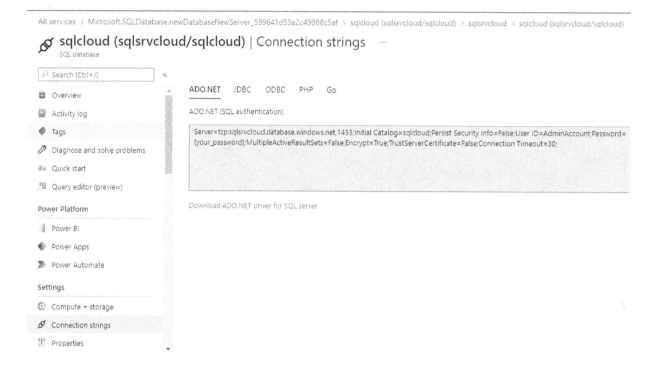

Exercise 11.3: Enable Azure AD Authentication for User2

In this exercise we will enable Azure Active Directory Authentication to SQL Database for Azure AD User User2. Azure AD User User2 was created in Exercise 8.3 in Chapter 8.

1. Go to Azure SQL database Server sqlsrvcloud dashboard and click Azure Active Directory in left pane> Note the Set admin option in right pane.

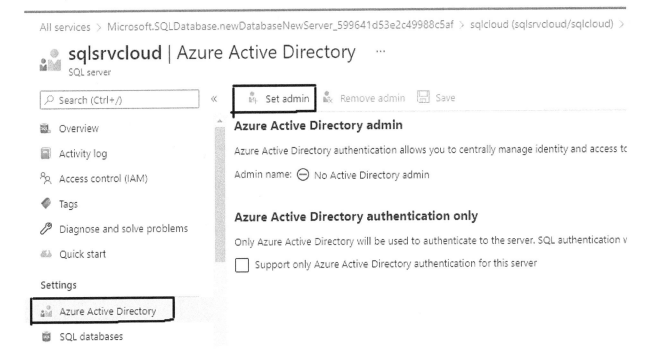

2. In above figure Click Set admin in Right pane>Azure Active Directory Add Admin Blade opens as shown below>In search Box type User >In Result Select User2> User2 will now appear under Selected item> Click Select.

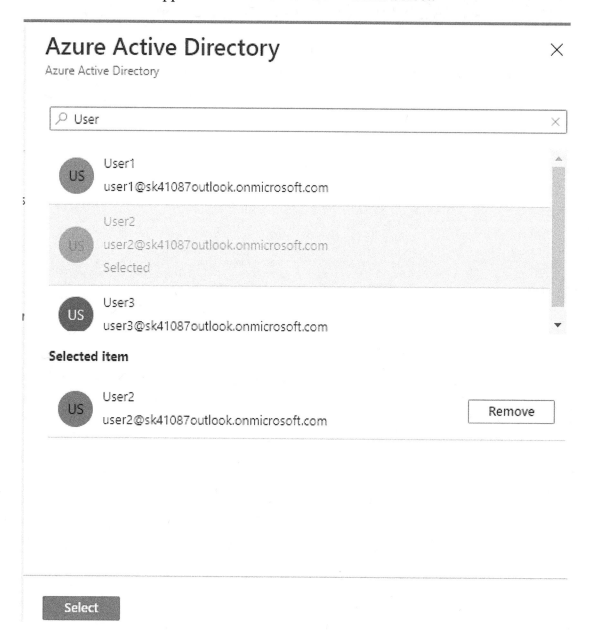

3. You are back in sqlsrvcloud Dashboard> Click **Save.** User2 will now be added as Azure Active Directory Admin. This will allow Azure Active Directory Authentication for User1.

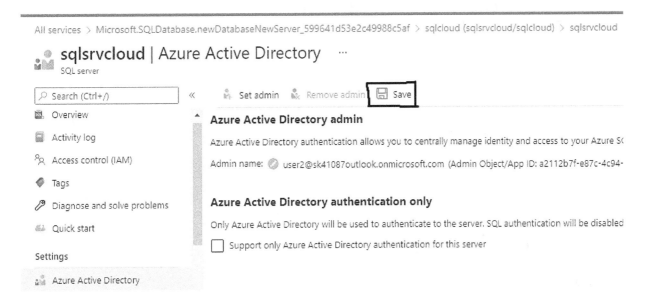

4. You can now see Green check mark against User2. This means User2 is now allowed for Azure Active Directory Authentication in Azure SQL Database Server sqlsrvcloud.

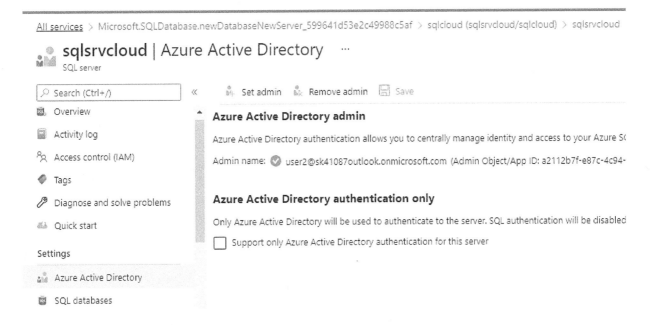

5. On the client machine whose IP was entered in step 9 of previous Exercise, open SSMS and enter Azure SQL database server name. In my case it was sqlsrvcloud.database.windows.net>In Authentication Select Active Directory Password>In Username enter user2@sk41087outlook.onmicrosoft.com> Enter password of User2 and click Connect.

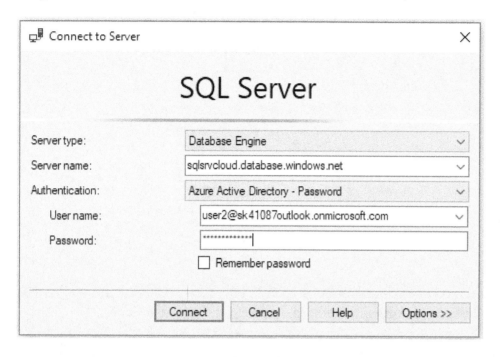

6. Figure below shows that User2 has successfully connected to Azure SQL Database Server sqlsrvcloud> Expand Database and you can see Azure SQL Database sqlcloud.

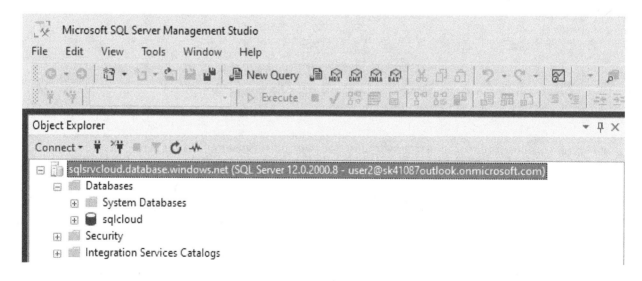

7. Close SQL Server Management Studio (SSMS) on your laptop.

Chapter 12 Azure App Services Web App

Introduction to Azure Web App

Azure App Services or Web Apps is a Multi-tenant Web App Service that is fully managed compute platform and is optimized for hosting websites and web applications.

Web Apps is a managed Windows VM with pre-installed IIS web server with a option to choose application framework (You can choose from Dot Net, PHP, Node.js, Python & Java) at Web App creation time.

(Note: In this chapter we will discuss Web App for windows only and not Web App for Linux).

The Diagram below shows the difference between Azure IaaS VM and Azure Web App. **The boxes with Dark grey color are managed by Azure Cloud (Imp Points).**

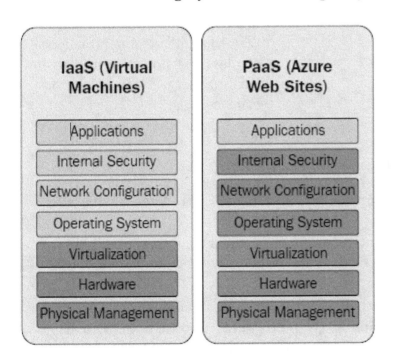

Using Web App you can develop in your favourite language, be it .NET, .NET Core, Java, Ruby, Node.js, PHP, or Python. Web Apps adds the power of Microsoft Azure services to your application, such as security, load balancing, autoscaling, and automated management.

Comparing Windows VM and Web Apps

Feature	Windows Azure VM	Web Apps
Deployment time	10-15 minutes	Within a minute
Pre-installed IIS Web Server and Application Framework	No	Yes
Available Option to choose for Application Framework	None	Dot Net, PHP, Node.js, Python & Java
Automatic OS updates, patches and security update by Azure team	No	Yes
Scale out without configuring any load balancer	No	Yes
Built in additional Features available with Web App only.		continuous integration and deployment, User authentication with Multiple identity providers, Deployment slot, Built in Website Performance Test, Built in Load Balancer

Web App Features

1. **Multiple languages and frameworks** - Support for ASP.NET, Node.js, Java, PHP, and Python.
2. **DevOps optimization** - Set up continuous integration and deployment with Visual Studio Team Services, GitHub, or BitBucket. Promote updates through test and staging environments.
3. **Global scale with high availability** - Scale-out manually or automatically.
4. **Connections to SaaS platforms and on-premises data** - Choose from more than 50 connectors for enterprise systems (such as SAP, Siebel, and Oracle), SaaS services (such as Salesforce and Office 365), and internet services (such as Facebook and Twitter). Access on-premises data using Hybrid Connections and Azure Virtual Networks.
5. **Security and compliance** - App Service is ISO, SOC, and PCI compliant.
6. **Visual Studio integration** - Dedicated tools in Visual Studio streamline the work of creating, deploying, and debugging.

App Service Plan

Each Web App is associated with App Service Plan. An App Service plan defines a features and set of compute resources available for a Web App to run.

To host Web Apps, Six Pricing tiers are available in App Service Plan: **Free, Shared, Basic, Standard, Premium and Isolated.**

Apps in the same subscription, region, and resource group can share an App Service plan. But individual Web App can be part of only one service plan.

All applications assigned to an **App Service plan** share the resources defined by it. This sharing saves money when hosting multiple apps in a single App Service plan.

	Free	Shared	Basic	Standard	Premium	Isolated
Web, mobile, or API apps	10	100	Unlimited	Unlimited	Unlimited	Unlimited
Disk space	1 GB	1 GB	10 GB	50 GB	250 GB	1 TB
Maximum instances	NA	NA	3	10	20	100
Deployment Slots	NA	NA	NA	Supported	Supported	Supported
Custom domain	NA	Supported	Supported	Supported	Supported	Supported
SSL			Supported	Supported	Supported	Supported
Hybrid Connections			Supported	Supported	Supported	Supported
Auto Scale	NA	NA	NA	Supported	Supported	Supported
VNET Connectivity	NA	NA	NA	Supported	Supported	Supported
Private Endpoints	NA	NA	NA	NA	Supported	Supported
Compute Type	Shared	Shared	Dedicated	Dedicated	Dedicated	Isolated
Use Cases	Trying out or Dev/Test	Dev/Test	Dedicated Test/Dev and low volume traffic	Production Workloads	Enhanced Performance for workloads	Scale, Security and Isolation

Exercise 12.1: Create Web App

In this exercise we will create Web App in Resource Group RGCloud and in Location **West US 2.** We will use system created Free App Service plan. Resource Group RGCloud was created in Exercise 4.1 in Chapter 4.

1. Open Chrome Browser and log on to Azure Portal @ portal.azure.com using Subscription Administrator credentials and password> Azure Portal opens as shown below. In Azure Portal Click 3 Horizontal lines in top left> A pane opens in left of Azure Portal as shown below> Note the **All services** option in left pane.

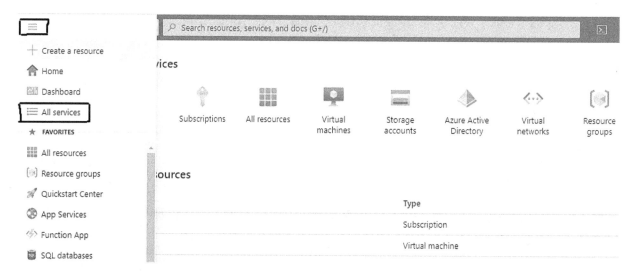

2. In Azure Portal Click All services in left pane> All Services pane opens as shown below> In All services pane click Web in left pane> In right pane note the App Service option.

3. In above figure click App Services >All App Services Pane opens as shown below> Note the + Create option.

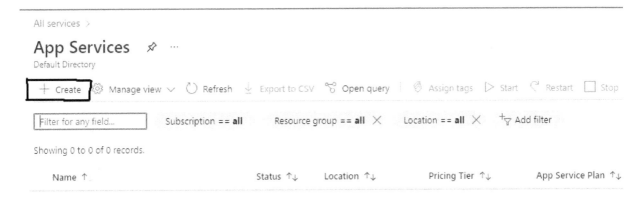

4. In above figure Click + Create> Create Web App blade opens as shown below> In Resource Group select RGCloud> Enter name for Web App> In Publish select Code> Select Runtime Stack as per your requirement. I selected ASP.NET V4.8> For OS select Windows> In Region select **West US 2**> System will automatically create Free App Service Plan> Click Review + create.

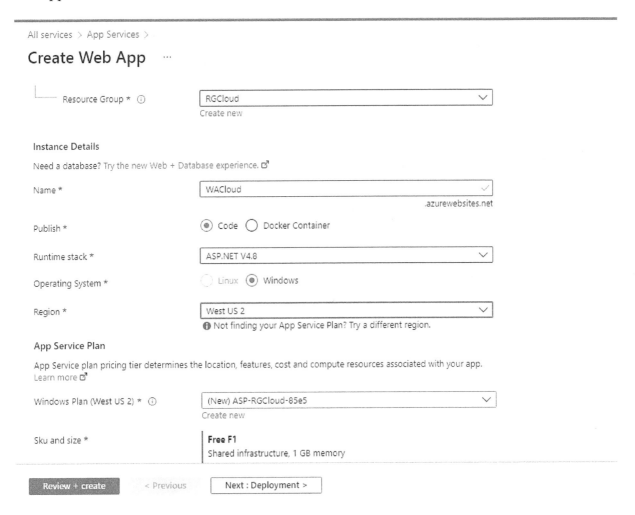

5. Review + create screen opens as shown below> Click Create (Not Shown).

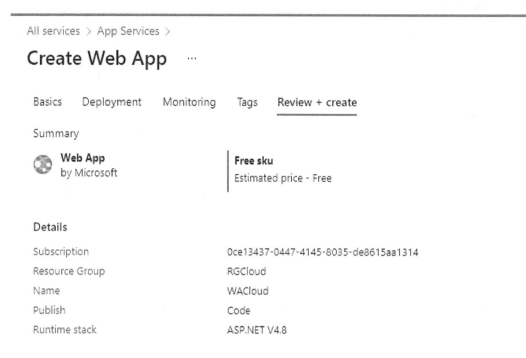

6. Figure bellows shows the Dashboard of Web App WACloud> Note the Web App URL in right pane. In my case it is https://wacloud.azurewebsites.net.

7. Copy DNS name of Web App (URL) from Right pane in above figure and open it in a Browser. Default Website opens as shown below.

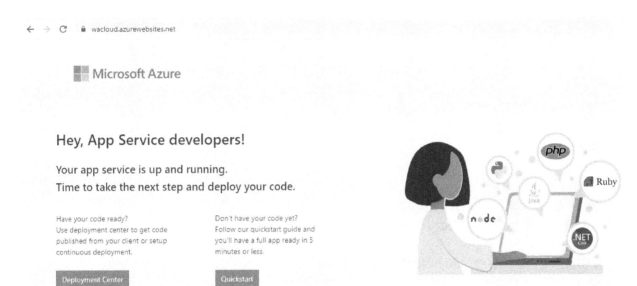

Website Authentication with Identity Providers

You can add authentication to Azure Web App website. Web App supports multiple authentication providers.

Web App Service supports following identity providers out of the box:

Azure Active Directory
Facebook
Google
Microsoft Account
Twitter
OpenID Connect provider (Preview)
Sign in with Apple provider (Preview)

Benefits of Web App Authentication Feature

1. The biggest benefit of Web App authentication feature is that you don't have to add any code in the application to enable Web App Authentication.

2. Another big benefit of Web App authentication feature is that it eliminates the overhead of creating and managing Identity Infrastructure.

Exercise 12.2: Enable Web App Authentication using Azure AD

In this exercise we will enable Authentication on Web App WACloud using Azure AD Option. To test the Authentication we will use Azure AD User User1. Web App WACloud was created in Exercise 12.1. Azure AD User User1 was created in Exercise 8.2 in Chapter 8.

1. In Web App WACloud Dashboard Click Authentication in left Pane> In right pane note the Add identity provider option.

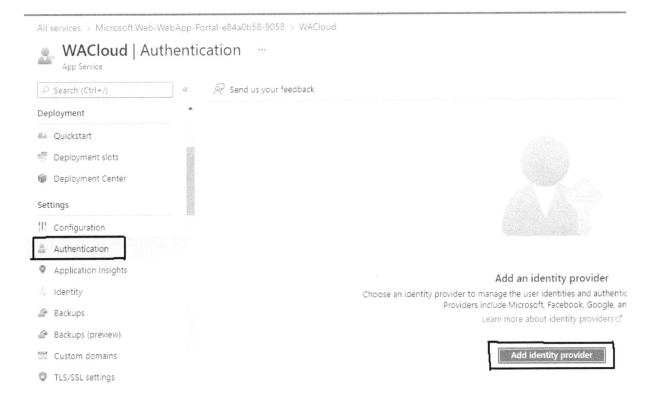

2. In above figure click Add identity provider in right pane> In Identity provider dropdown box select Microsoft> Rest select all default Values> Click Add.

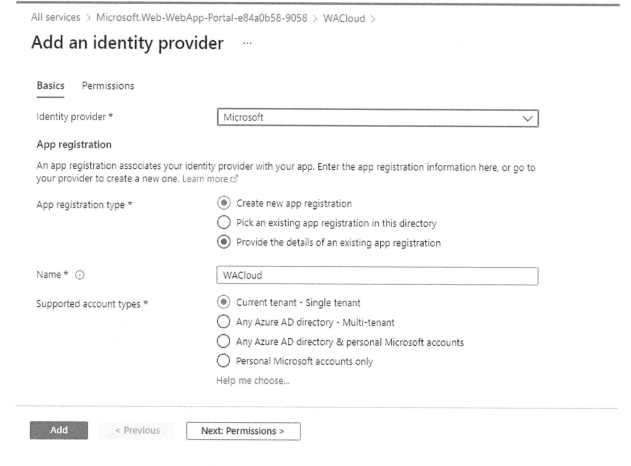

3. You will be back in Web App WACloud Dashboard with Authentication selected in left pane.

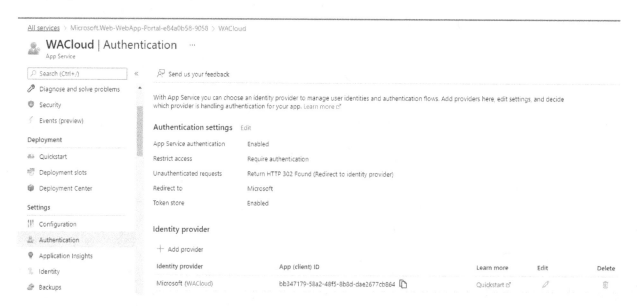

4. **Open Firebox browser** and enter DNS name of Web App WACloud. In my case URL is: https://wacloud.azurewebsites.net. Website is asking for authentication. I entered User1 credentials – user1@sk41087outlook.onmicrosoft.com and password. Azure AD user User1 was created in Exercise 7.1 in Chapter 7.

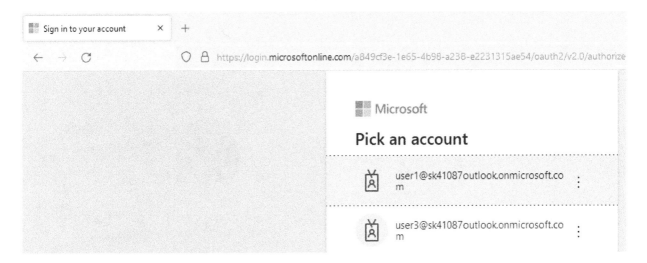

5. Permission request pane pops up> Click Accept.

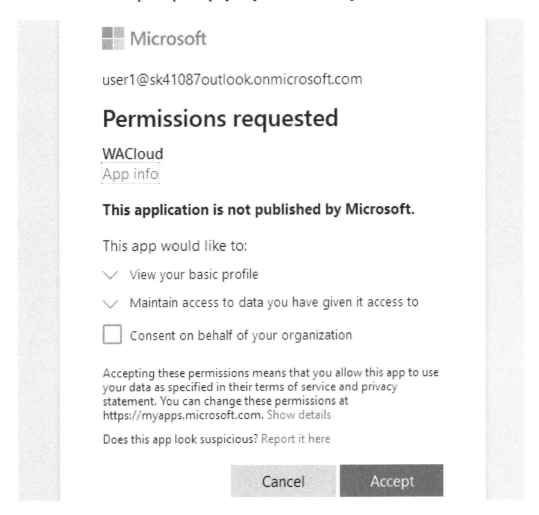

6. After Authentication Web App WACloud default website opens as shown below.

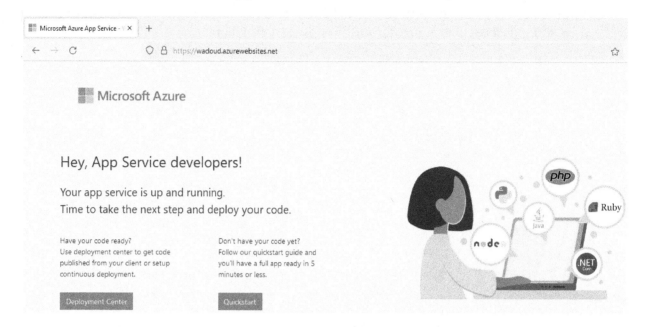

From above you can see that you can enable authentication on Web App without adding any code in the application.

Exercise 12.3: Disable Web App Authentication

1. Go to Web App WACloud Dashboard and click Authentication in left pane>In Right pane Click Delete icon under Delete column> Delete identity provider pane pops up. Click Delete.

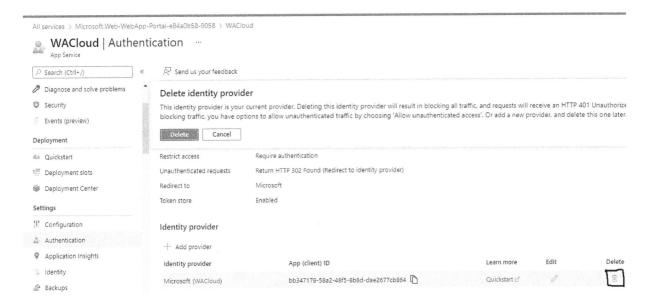

2. Remove authentication box pops up> Click Remove Authentication.

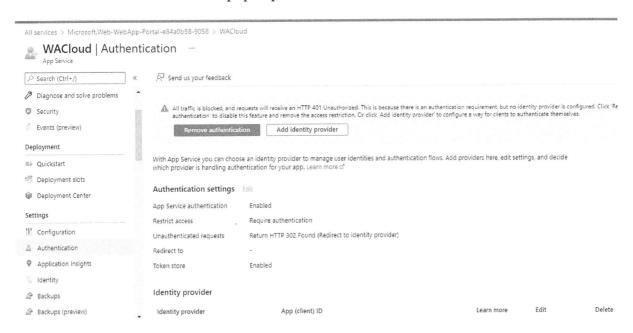

Exercise 12.4: Custom Website Code

In this Exercise we will create Custom Website code. In upcoming Exercise 12.6 we will upload Custom Website code to Web App WACloud created in Exercise 12.1.

1. On your laptop/Desktop open Notepad and enter following:

```
<!DOCTYPE html>
<html>
<head>
<title>Azure Guide</title>
<meta charset="utf-8">
</head>
<body>
<h1>Azure Study & Lab Guide for Beginners</h1>
<p> Author: Harinder Kohli </p>
</body>
</html>
```

2. Save the file as index.html on your laptop/desktop.

Exercise 12.5: Create FTP Credentials

We will use FTP user to deploy Custom Website code to Web App wacloud. To create FTP credentials we have 2 options. We can either use System created FTP credentials or User created FTP Credentials. In this lab will copy system created FTP credentials.

1. Go to Web App WACloud Dashboard> Click Deployment Center in left pane> In Right pane click FTPS credentials> In right pane note the **FTPS endpoint, Username and Password option.**

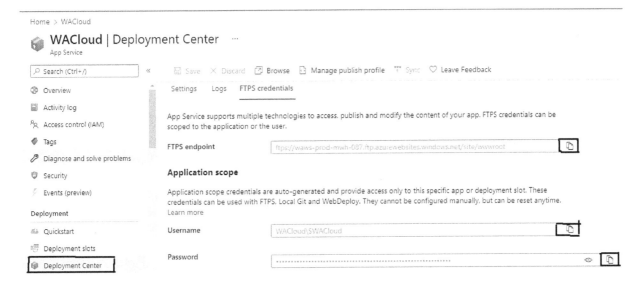

2. Open Notepad on your laptop/Desktop. Copy FTPS endpoint, Username and Password using copy button and Paste them in Notepad.

Exercise 12.6: Upload index.html to Web App wacloud using FileZilla

In this Exercise we will upload Custom website code created in Exercise 12.4 to Web App wacloud. Note that Custom website code was saved as index.html on our laptop. To log on to Web App wacloud we will use FTP credentials copied in previous Exercise.

1. Download & Install FileZilla client from
   https://filezilla-project.org/download.php?platform=win64

2. Open FileZilla Client> In Host enter FTPS endpoint value copied from previous Exercise> In Username enter value copied from previous Exercise> In Password enter value copied from previous Exercise> Leave Port option as blank> Click Quickconnect.

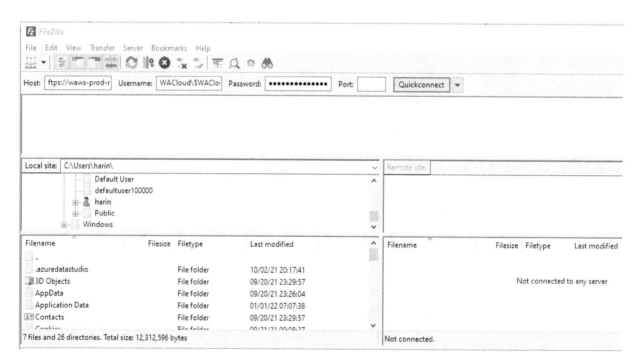

3. After connection is established following pane comes up> Note the Remote site option> click **+Site in right pane to expand it** >Click wwwroot>You can see the default website html file hostingstart.html in bottom pane.

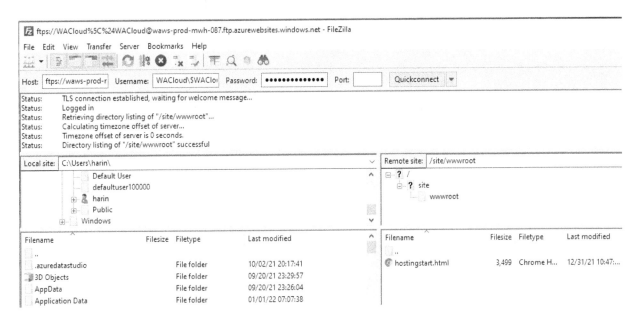

4. We will now drag index.html file (Created in Exercise 11.4) from our laptop/desktop to wwwroot folder. You can now see index.html file in bottom pane.

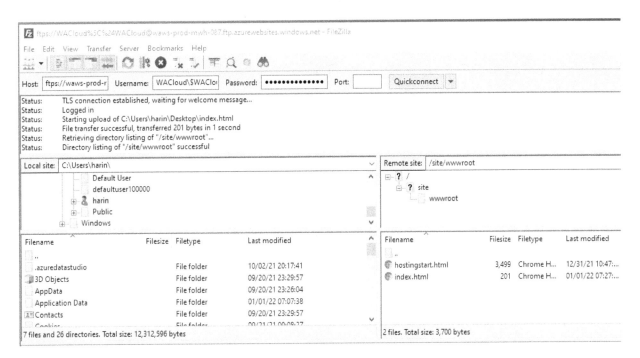

5. Open Browser and enter DNS name of Web App wacloud. You can now see the Custom Website. If required press f5 on your laptop/Desktop.

Azure Study & Lab Guide for Beginners

Author: Harinder Kohli

6. Instead of Default web site hostingstart.html we now have index.html.

Chapter 13 Load Balancing

Azure Load Balancing Overview

Load balancing distributes traffic across multiple endpoints.

Microsoft Azure offers four types of load Balancers: Azure Front Door, Azure Load Balancer, Application Gateway & Traffic Manager.

Azure Front Door provides **Multi-Region** HTTP/HTTPS Load Balancing and high availability to your Web Applications. Azure Front Door deals with web traffic only (HTTP/HTTPS/WebSocket).

Azure Load Balancer is a Layer 4 (TCP, UDP) load balancer that distributes incoming traffic among healthy instances defined in a load-balanced set.

Application Gateway works at the application layer (Layer 7). Application Gateway deals with web traffic only (HTTP/HTTPS/WebSocket).

Traffic Manager works at the DNS level. It uses DNS responses to direct end-user traffic to globally distributed endpoints. Clients then connect to those endpoints directly.

Global v/s Regional Load Balancing

Global Load Balancing service load balances traffic between endpoints which are hosted across different regions/geographies. These services route end-user traffic to the closest available backend. They also react to changes in service reliability or performance, in order to maximize availability and performance.

Regional load-balancing services distribute traffic within virtual networks across virtual machines (VMs) or zonal and zone-redundant service endpoints within a region. You can think of them as systems that load balance between VMs, containers, or clusters within a region in a virtual network.

HTTP(S) versus non-HTTP(S) Load Balancing Services

HTTP(S) load-balancing services are Layer 7 load balancers that only accept HTTP(S) traffic. They are intended for web applications.
Non-HTTP/S load-balancing services can handle both HTTPS & non-HTTP(S) traffic, but they are recommended for non-web workloads.

Table below summarizes the Azure load balancing services.

Service	Global/Regional	Recommended Traffic
Azure Front Door	Global	HTTPS
Traffic Manager	Global	Non-HTTPS
Application Gateway	Regional	HTTPS
Azure Load Balancer	Regional	Non-HTTPS
Azure Load Balancer	Global	Non-HTTPS

Exercise 13.1: Load Balancing Virtual Machines vmcloud2 and vmcloud1

In this exercise we will create Azure Load Balancer Standard in Resource Group RGCloud and in Region East US 2. Azure Load Balancer will Load Balance Virtual Machines vmcloud2 and vmcloud1. Resource Group RGCloud was created in Exercise 4.1 in Chapter 4. Virtual Machines vmcloud2 and vmcloud1 were created in Chapter 6.

1. Open Chrome Browser and log on to Azure Portal @ portal.azure.com using Subscription Administrator credentials and password> Azure Portal opens as shown below. In Azure Portal Click 3 Horizontal lines in top left> A pane opens in left of Azure Portal as shown below> Note the **All services** option in left pane.

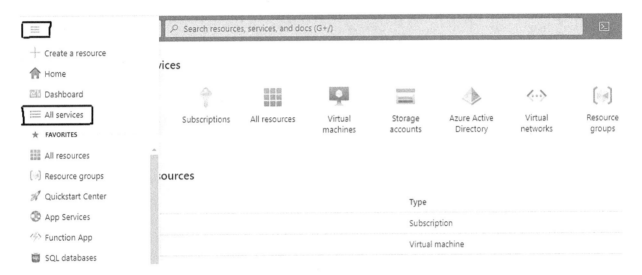

1. In Azure Portal Click All services in left pane> All Services pane opens as shown below> In All services pane click Networking in left pane> In right pane note the Load balancers option.

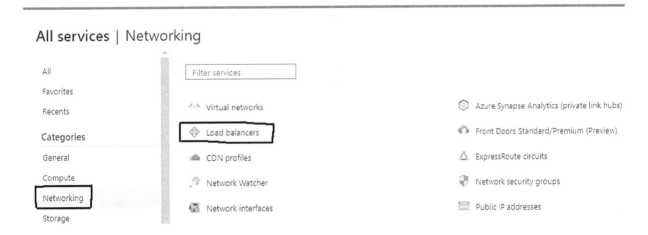

Azure Study & Lab Guide For Beginners

2. In above figure click Load balancers> All Load Balancer Pane opens as shown below> Note the + Create option.

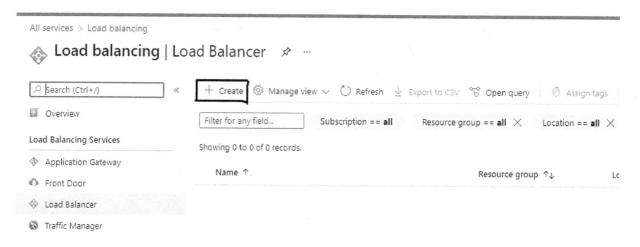

3. In above figure Click + Create> Create Load balancer blade opens as shown below> In Resource Group select RGCloud> Enter name> In Region select East US 2> In SKU select Standard> In type select Public> In Tier select Regional> Click Next: Frontend IP configuration.

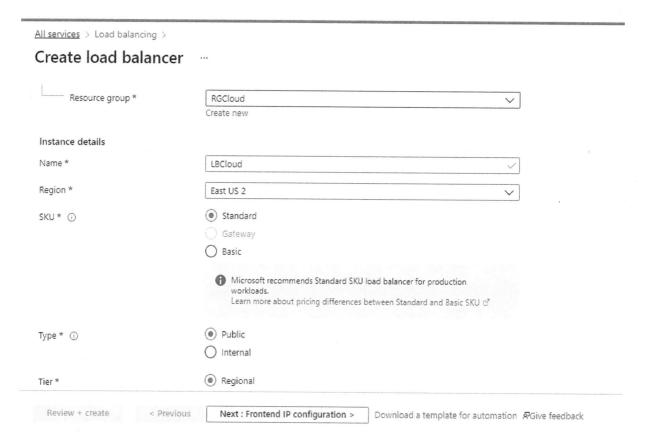

4. Frontend IP configuration pane opens as shown below> Note the + Add a frontend IP configuration option.

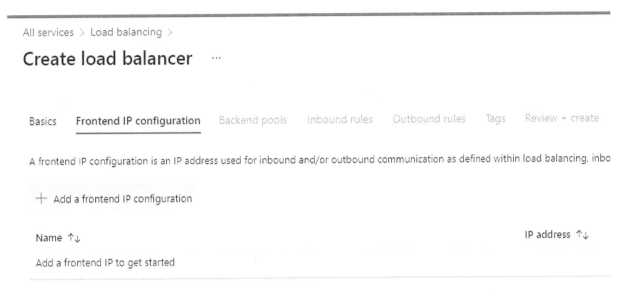

5. In above figure click + Add a frontend IP configuration> Add frontend IP address blade opens as shown below> Enter Name> In IP version select IPv4> In IP type select IP address> Note link **Create new** in Public IP address.

6. In above figure click link **Create new**> Add a public IP address blade opens as shown below> Enter name> In Availability zone select No Zone> Click OK.

7. You will be back in Add frontend IP address blade > Click Add.

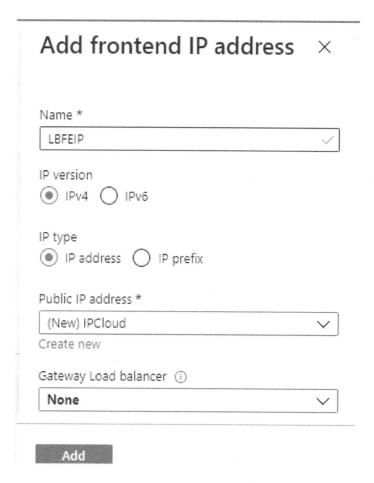

8. You will be back in Frontend IP configuration pane> Click Next: Backend pools.

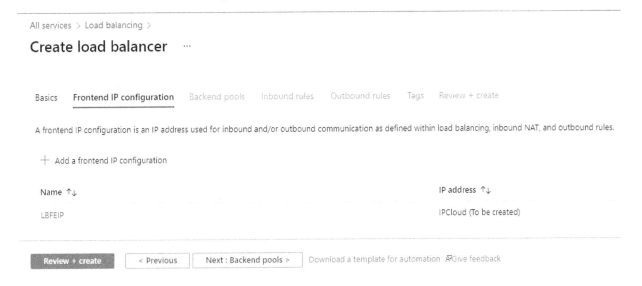

9. Backend pools pane opens as shown below> Note the + Add a backend pool option.

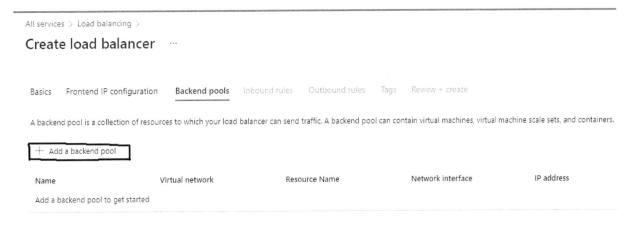

10. In above figure click + Add a backend pool> Add backend pool blade opens as shown below> Enter a name> In Virtual Network select VNETCloud> Select IP Address in Backend pool Configuration> In IP Address column select VM vmcloud2 private IP> In IP Address column select VM vmcloud1 private IP> Click Add.

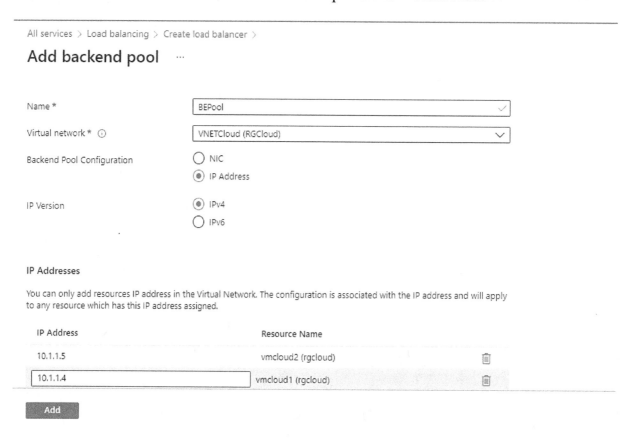

11. You will be back in Backend pools pane as shown below> It shows Backend pool BEPool with 2 Virtual Machines added> Click Next: Inbound rules.

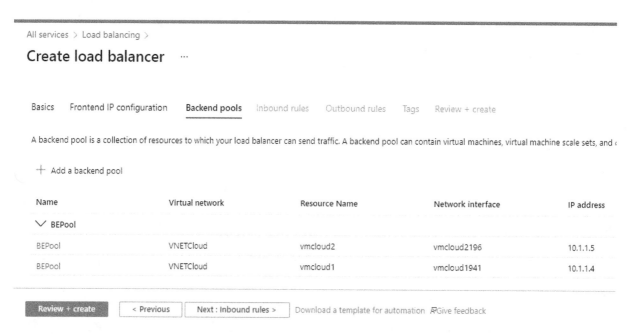

Azure Study & Lab Guide For Beginners

12. Inbound rules pane opens > Note the option + Add a load balancing rule.

13. In above figure click + Add a load balancing rule> Add load balancing rule blade opens as shown below> Enter name> In Frontend IP address select LBFEIP created in Step 5> In Backend pool select BEPool created in step 10> In Port and Backend Port enter 80> In Health Probe note the link Create new.

14. In above figure click Create new> Add health probe blade opens as shown below>
Enter a name> In Protocol select HTTP> Rest Select all default values> Click OK.

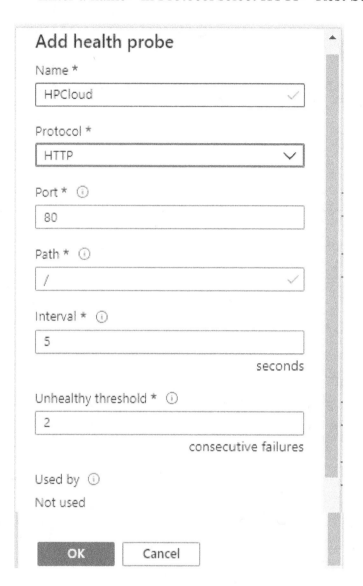

15. You will be back in Add load balancing rule blade> In idle timeout enter 15> In TCP Reset select Enabled> Select Use implicit outbound rule> Click Add.

16. You will be back in Inbound rules pane> Click Review + Create

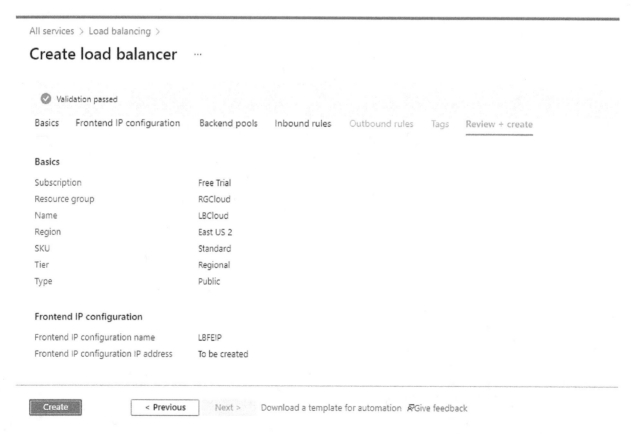

17. Review + create screen opens as shown below> Click Create.

18. Figure below shows Dashboard of Load Balancer> Note the Frontend IP configuration option in left pane.

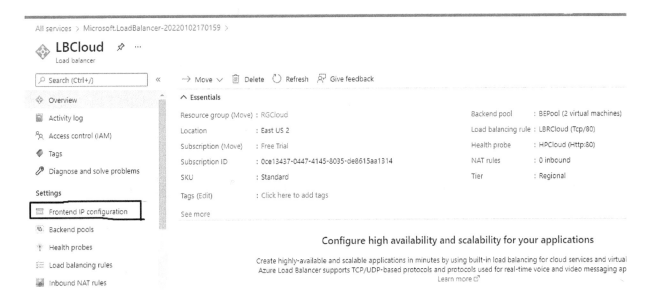

19. In above figure click Frontend IP configuration > In Frontend IP configuration note the IP Address assigned to Load Balancer. In my case it is 20.114.224.98. In Book Readers case IP Address will be different.

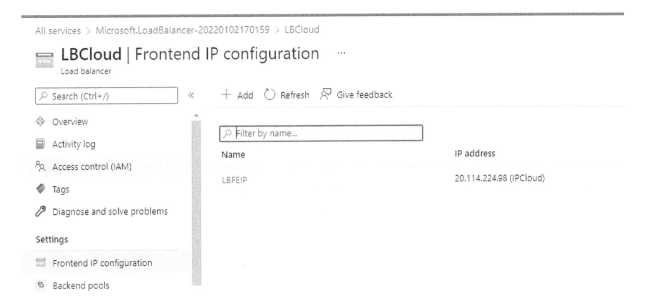

20. Open Firefox Browser and enter 20.114.224.98> Default Website on VM vmcloud1 opens as shown below.

21. On your laptop refresh the page by pressing F5 couple of times> Custom Website on VM vmcloud2 opens as shown below.

Azure Study & Lab Guide for Beginners

Author: Harinder Kohli

Chapter 14 Azure Backup and Recovery

Azure Backup is Backup as a service (BaaS) which you can use to backup your data in Azure cloud.
You can backup both Azure Cloud workloads and On-premises workloads.
Azure Backups are stored in Recovery Services Vault or Backup Vault.
Advantage of Azure backup is that we don't have to set up Backup infrastructure.

Backup Data Location

Backup Data Location can be **Recovery Services Vault** or **Backup Vault** in Azure Cloud.

Recovery Services Vault (RSV)

A Recovery Services Vault is a storage entity in Azure that houses backup data.

You can use Recovery Services Vault to hold backup data for on-premises workload and for various Azure services such as IaaS VMs (Linux or Windows) and Azure SQL Server VMs.

Backup scenarios with Azure Backup

Azure Backup provides following 4 options to Backup Cloud and on-premises workloads to Recovery Services Vault in Azure Cloud.

- Microsoft Azure Recovery Services (MARS) Agent
- Azure IaaS VM Backup using Backup Extension Agent
- System Center DPM Server + MARS Agent
- Microsoft Azure Backup Server (MABS) + MARS Agent

Note: In this Book we will focus on Recovery Services Vault (RSV) only.

Azure IaaS VM Backup using Backup Extension Agent

Azure IaaS VM Backup provides Native backups for Azure Windows/Linux VMs. This option can be used to backup Azure VMs only. The benefit of this option is that Backup option is built in VM dashboard.

Backup to Azure requires following components

1. Recovery services Vault.
2. Azure Backup Extension Agent. Azure backup agent extension is automatically enabled when backup is enabled on the VM.

Azure IaaS Windows VM Backup Working

The Backup service uses the *VMSnapshot*extension to backup workloads. The Backup service coordinates with the Volume Shadow Copy Service (VSS) to get a consistent snapshot of the virtual machine's disks. Once the Azure Backup service takes the snapshot, the data is transferred to the vault.

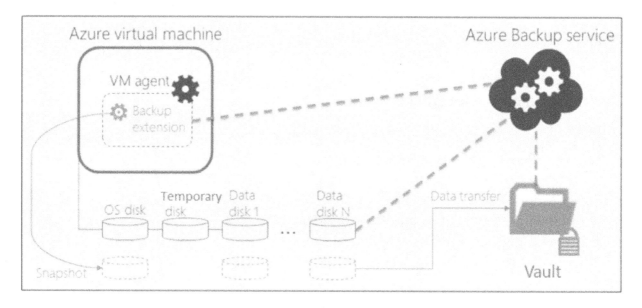

Architecture of Azure Backup using MARS Agent

Microsoft Azure Recovery Services (MARS) Agent backs up files and folders on Window server or Azure Windows VM to Recovery Services Vault in Azure. MARS Agent option can be used to backup both Cloud workloads and on-premises.

Backup to Azure requires following components.
• Recovery Services Vault.
• Microsoft Azure Recovery Services (MARS) Agent.

Mars Agent can backup following workloads

• Files & Folders: Azure Backup agent backs up files and folders in **on-premises** Window server and **Azure Cloud** Windows VMs to Recovery Services Vault.
• Windows System State.

Backup Location

Backs up data to Recovery Services Vault in Azure. There is no option to backup Data locally.

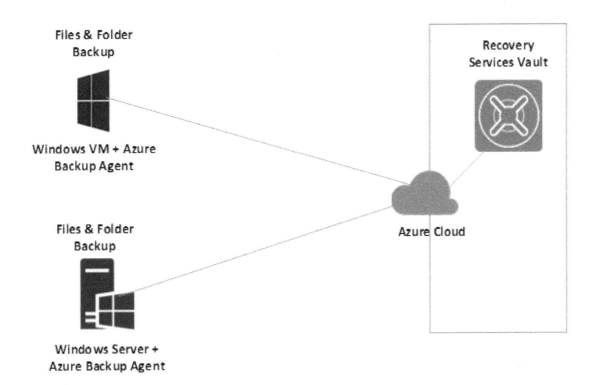

Backup Policy

A backup policy defines a matrix of when the data snapshots are taken and how long those snapshots are retained. Backup Policy has two components: **Schedule** (when to take Backup) and **Retention** (how long to retain Backup).

A **default back policy** is applied when you create Backup job. With Default Policy Backup is taken at Pre-defined time decided by the Azure System. Backup is retained for 30 days.

You can also create a **Custom Policy** according to your specific requirements. You can create Custom policy based on the type of data that's being backed up, RTO/RPO requirements, operational or regulatory compliance needs and workload type (VMs, Databases or Files).

Exercise 14.1: Create Recovery Services Vault

In this exercise we will create **Recovery Services Vault** in **Region East US 2** and in **Resource Group RGCloud.** Resource Group RGCloud was created in Exercise 4.1 in Chapter 4.

1. Open Chrome Browser and log on to Azure Portal @ portal.azure.com using Subscription Administrator credentials and password> Azure Portal opens as shown below. In Azure Portal Click 3 Horizontal lines in top left> A pane opens in left of Azure Portal as shown below> Note the **All services** option in left pane.

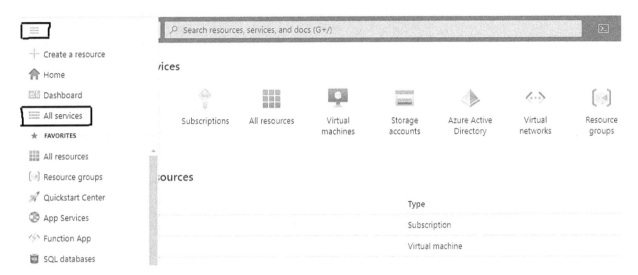

2. In Azure Portal Click All services in left pane> All Services pane opens as shown below> In All services pane click Storage in left pane> In right pane note the Recovery Services vaults option.

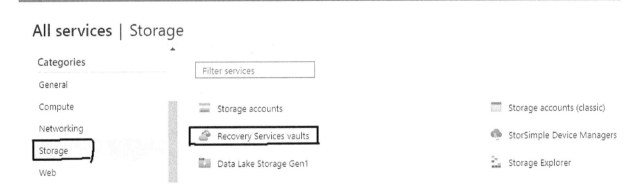

Note: Placement of Recovery Services vaults option in right pane might be different in Book Readers case.

3. In above figure click Recovery Services vaults> All Recovery Services vaults Pane opens as shown below> Note the + Create option.

4. In above figure Click + Create> Create Recovery Services vaults blade opens as shown below> In Resource Group select RGCloud> Enter a vault name. I entered **CloudVault**> In Region select East US 2> Click Review + Create.

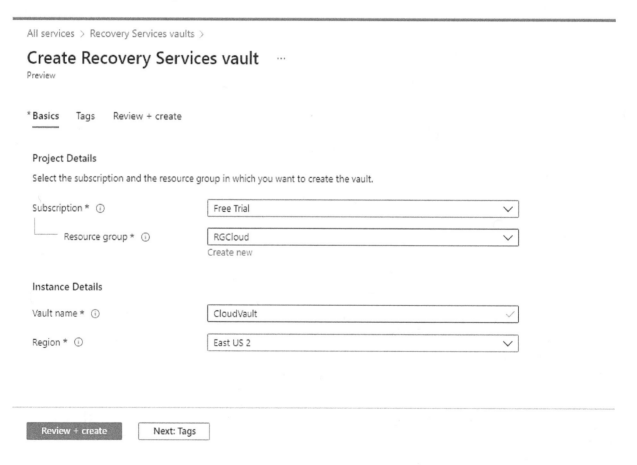

5. Review + create screen opens as shown below> Click Create.

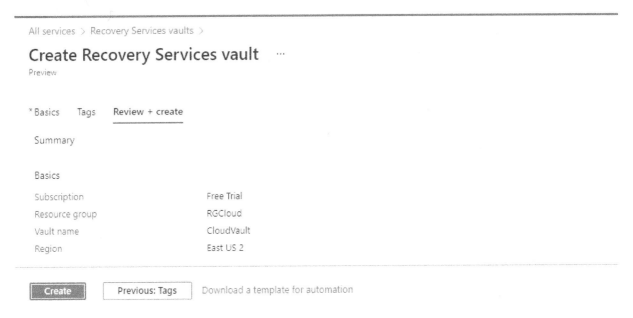

6. Figure below shows the Dashboard of Recovery Services Vault CloudVault> Note the Backup option in left pane. We will use this option in next Exercise to backup Virtual Machine vmcloud1.

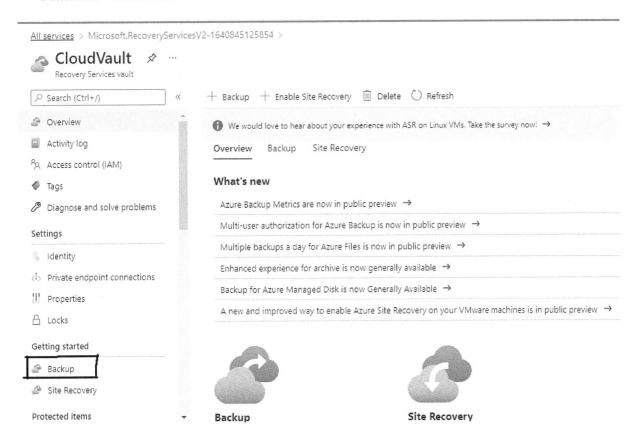

Exercise 14.2: Azure VM-level backup

In this exercise we will take Backup of Virtual Machine vmcloud2. Virtual Machine vmcloud2 was created in Exercise 6.5 in Chapter 6.

1. In Recovery Services Vault CloudVault dashboard Click Backup in left pane> Backup pane opens as shown below> In where is your workload running dropdown box select Azure> In what do you want to backup box select Virtual Machine.

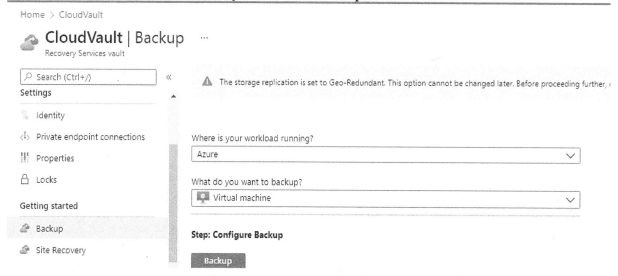

2. In above figure under Configure Backup click Backup> Configure Backup pane opens as shown below> Note the Backup Frequency daily @ 4 PM UTC. The Backup frequency is Pre-defined by Default Policy> Note the Add option.

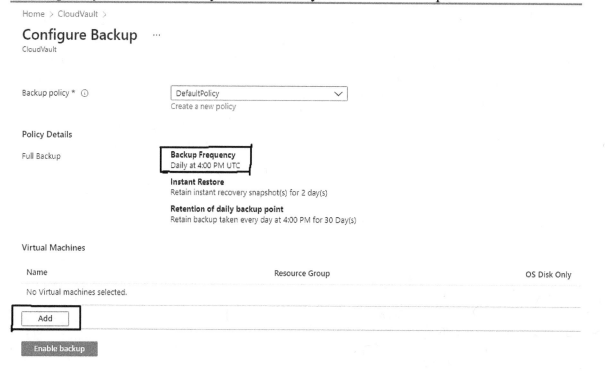

3. In above figure Click Add> Select Virtual Machine pane opens as shown below> Select VM vmcloud2> Click OK> You will be back in Configure Backup pane> Click Enable Backup.

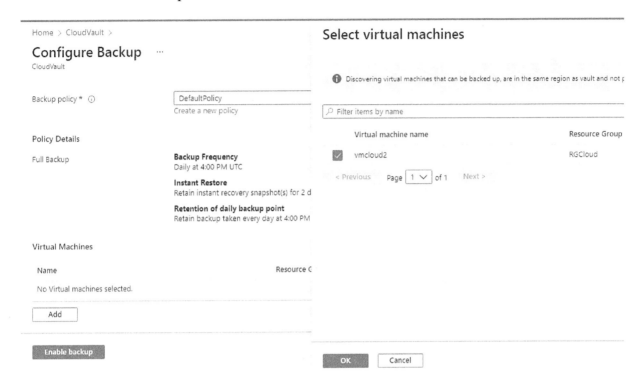

4. Configure Protection pane will open> Wait for the deployment to complete> It will take 1-2 minutes for deployment to complete.

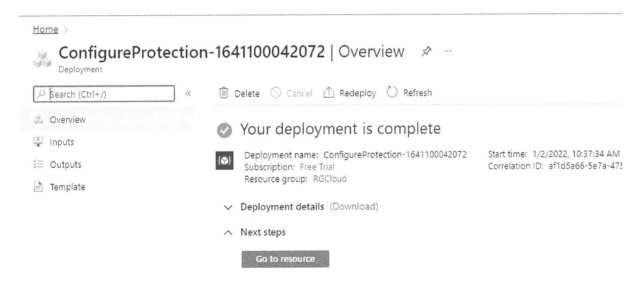

5. Click link Go to resource in above figure> You will be taken back to Recovery Services Vault CloudVault dashboard> In Recovery Services Vault CloudVault dashboard Click Backup items in left pane> In right pane note the Azure Virtual Machine option.

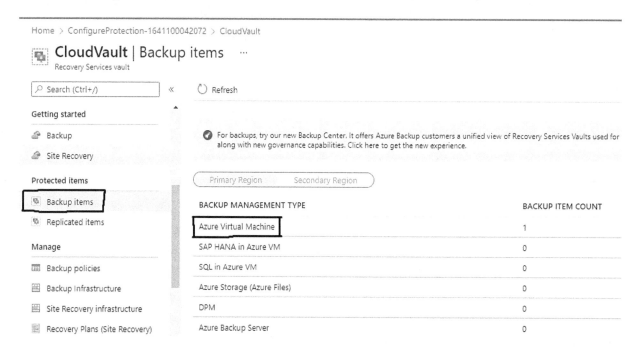

6. In above figure click Azure Virtual Machine in right pane> In Last Backup Status column you can see that **Initial Backup is pending.**

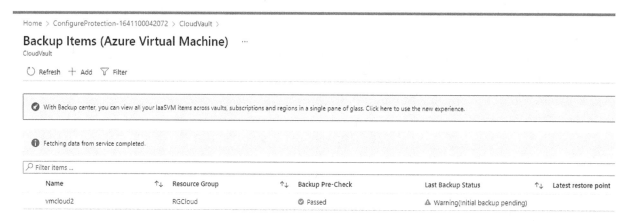

7. In above figure click the Row containing VM vmcloud2> VM vmcloud2 backup item pane opens as shown below> Note the option **Backup now.**

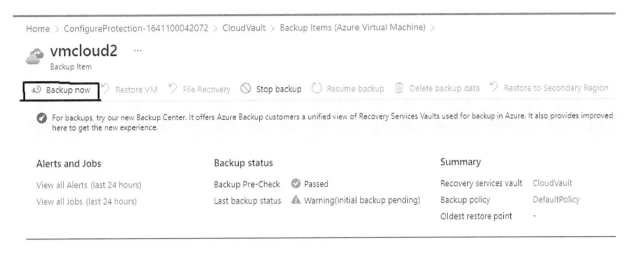

8. In above figure click Backup now> Backup Now pane opens as shown below> Click OK> On-demand Backup will be triggered.

9. You will be back in VM vmcloud2 backup item pane as shown below> Note the View all Jobs option.

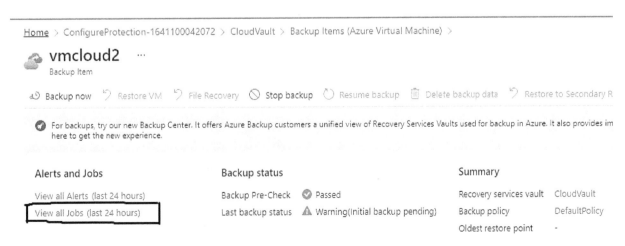

10. In above figure click View all jobs> Backup Jobs pane opens as shown below> In Second Row you can see that in Status column shows Backup is in Progress. Initial Backup will take time. We will come back to this pane after 2-3 hours.

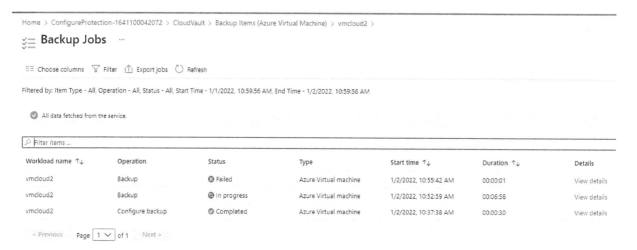

11. Just keep refreshing the backup job pane. You can see that initial backup job is completed. It took 1.01 hours to complete> Note the View details option.

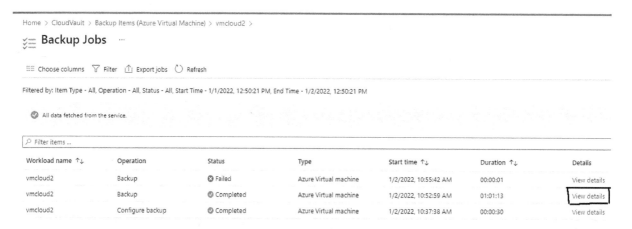

12. In above figure click View details to get details about the Backup.

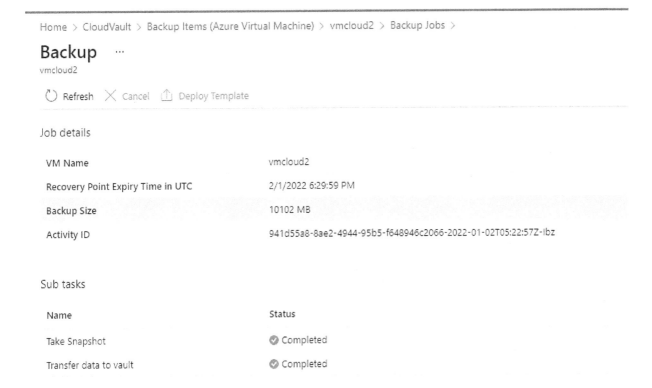

13. Close all the Backup panes.

14. Go to VM vmcloud2 dashboard and stop the VM.

Chapter 15 Azure Management

In Azure Cloud you get multiple options to Monitor, Manage and Protect Azure Resources.

- Azure Monitor
- Microsoft Defender for Cloud
- Microsoft Sentinel
- Azure Advisor
- Service Health

In this Chapter we will focus on Azure Monitor & Microsoft Defender for Cloud only.

Note: Make sure that VMs vmcloud1 and vmcloud2 are started before you start lab Exercises in this Chapter.

Azure Monitor

Azure Monitor is a comprehensive solution for **Collecting, Analyzing,** and **Acting** on telemetry data of your Azure Cloud and On-premises environment.

As shown below Azure Monitor collects Data from various sources such as Applications, Operating System & Azure Resources etc. Data Collected is then populated into Metrics and Log Data Store. Azure Monitor can then perform various actions on this collected data such as Alerting, Analysing with Log Analytics and Visualising etc.

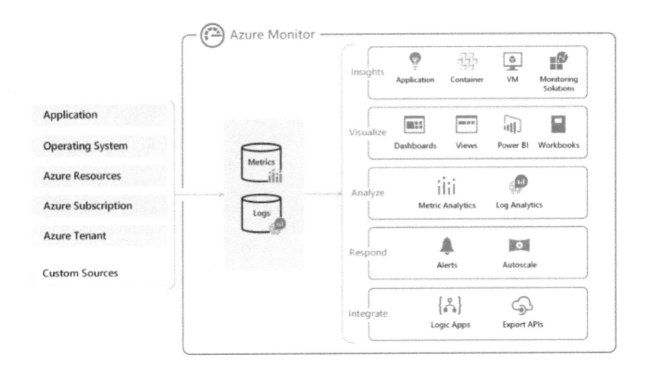

All data collected by Azure Monitor fits into one of two fundamental types - Metrics and Logs.

Metrics are numerical values that describe some aspect of a system at a particular point in time. They are lightweight and capable of supporting near real-time scenarios. **Logs** contain different kinds of data organized into records with different sets of properties for each type. Telemetry such as events and traces are stored as logs in addition to performance data so that it can all be combined for analysis.

Important Note: You can monitor resource through resource Dashboard or through Monitor Dashboard by selecting that particular resource.

Exercise 15.1: Accessing Monitor Dashboard

1. Open Chrome Browser and log on to Azure Portal @ portal.azure.com using Subscription Administrator credentials and password> Azure Portal opens as shown below. In Azure Portal Click 3 Horizontal lines in top left> A pane opens in left of Azure Portal as shown below> Note the **All services** option in left pane.

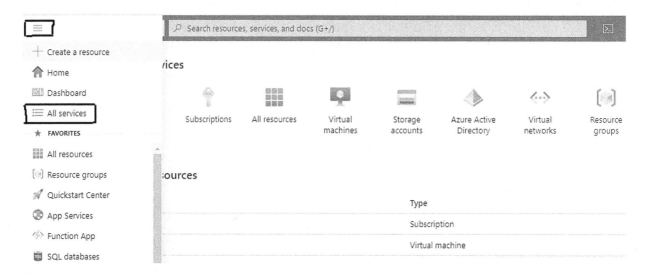

2. In Azure Portal Click All services in left pane> All Services pane opens as shown below> In All services pane scroll down in left pane till you see Monitor option> In right pane note the Monitor option.

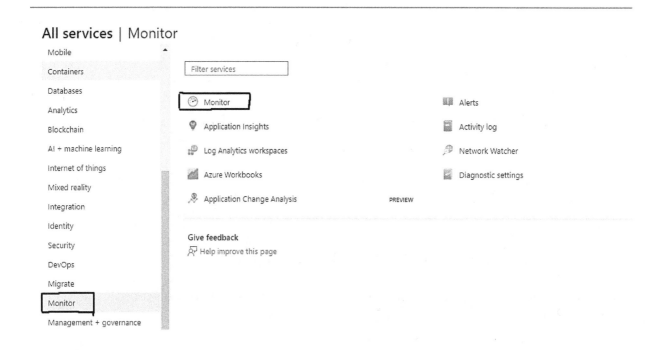

3. In above click Monitor in right pane> Monitor Dashboard opens as shown below.

Activity Log option provides control plane events on a resource. Activity Logs provide data about the operations on a resource from the outside.

Metrics are numerical values that describe some aspect of a system at a particular point in time.

Logs contain data about resource such as event & Performance data which can be queried for Analysis.

Service Health provides status of Azure services which can affect your business critical applications.

Workbooks combine text, Analytics queries, Azure Metrics, and parameters into rich interactive reports.

Applications is a Performance Management (APM) service for web applications. It monitor's live Web Application for availability, performance, and usage.

Note: Readers are requested to explore options in the left pane.

Exercise 15.2: Virtual Machine vmcloud1 CPU Metrics

You can view Virtual Machine Metrics using Monitor Dashboard or Virtual Machine Dashboard. In this Exercise we will use Virtual Machine vmcloud1 dashboard.

1. Go to Virtual Machine vmcloud1 dashboard> Scroll down in left pane and click Metrics> Metrics pane opens in right side as shown below> Click Metrics Dropdown box and you can see various Metric options for Virtual Machine> Scroll down and you can see Percentage CPU option.

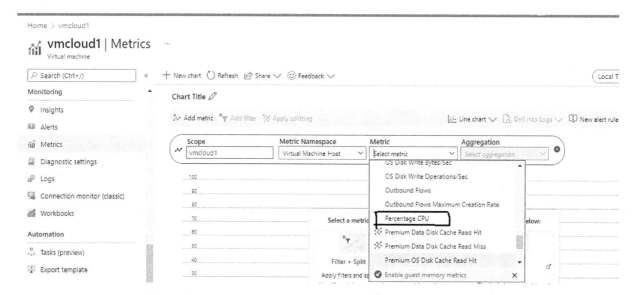

2. In above figure click Percentage CPU in Metric dropdown box> Percentage CPU Graph opens below.
    Note: Metric Percentage CPU refers to Percentage of allocated compute units that are currently in use by the Virtual Machine.

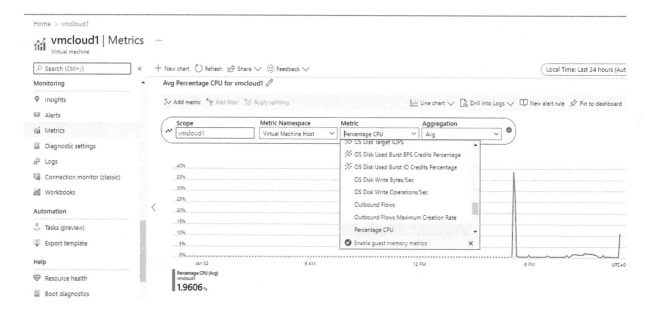

Exercise 15.3: Activity Log

Activity Log option provides control plane events on a resource. Activity Logs provide data about the operations on a resource from the outside. You can view Activity logs using Monitor Dashboard or Resource Dashboard. In this Exercise we will use Monitor dashboard to view Activity logs of Virtual Machine vmcloud1.

1. In Monitor dashboard Click Activity log in left pane> Activity Log pane opens as shown below> By default it gives information on Activity Logs for all the Resources for last 6 Hours.

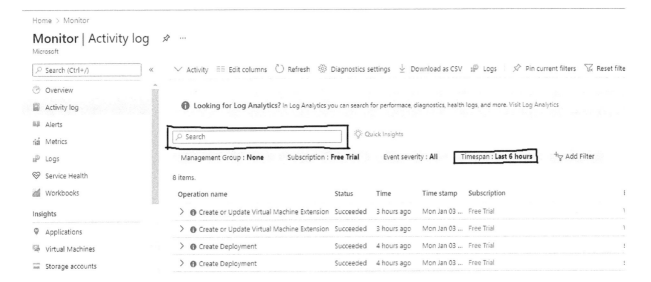

2. In above figure click Timespan box> A dropdown pane opens. Select Last 2 weeks> Click Apply.

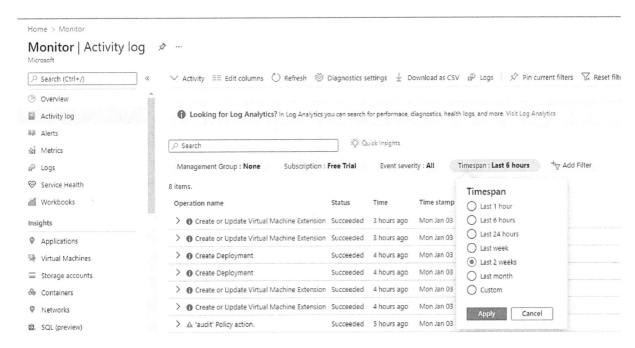

3. You can now see Activity Logs for all the Resources for last 2 Weeks.

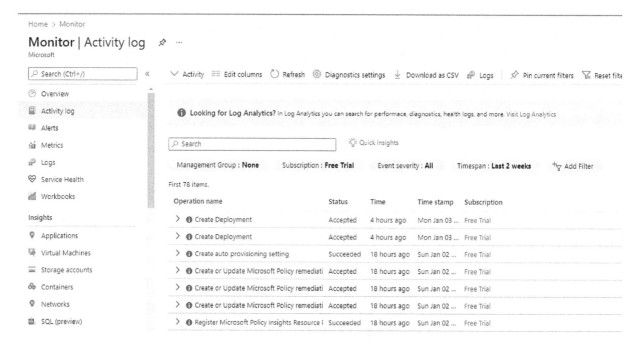

4. In above figure in search pane enter vmcloud1> You can Activity Logs of VM vmcloud1.

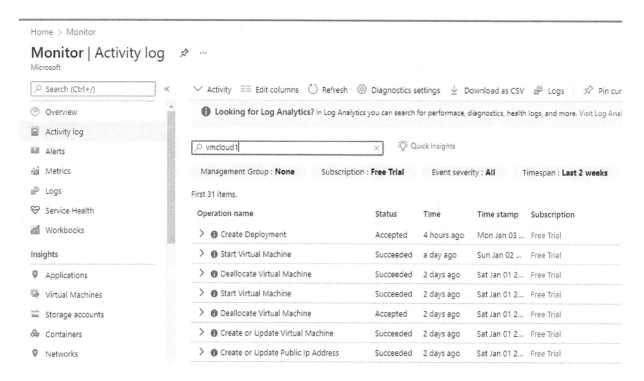

Microsoft Defender for Cloud

Microsoft Defender for Cloud collects security data and events from Azure Cloud and On-premises resources and services to help you prevent, detect, and respond to threats.

Microsoft Defender for Cloud is an Azure Managed Service that **detects** threats against your Azure resources and Non Azure Resources and helps you to **remediate** those threats.

Microsoft Defender for Cloud can be used to monitor your infrastructure as a service (IaaS) resources such as Azure Virtual Machines, PaaS resources such as Azure SQL Database and Non Azure Resources like on-premises servers.

Microsoft Defender for Cloud Tiers

Microsoft Defender for Cloud is offered in two tiers: Free and Paid. Microsoft Defender for Cloud is free for the first 30 days. Any usage beyond 30 days will be automatically charged.

Table below shows comparison between Free Tier and Paid Tiers.

Feature	Free	Paid
Continuous assessment and security recommendations	✓	✓
Azure secure score	✓	✓
Just in time VM Access	NA	✓
Adaptive application controls and Network Hardening	NA	✓
Regulatory compliance dashboard and reports	NA	✓
Threat protection for Azure VMs and non-Azure servers (Including server EDR)	NA	✓
Threat protection for supported PaaS services	NA	✓

Free tier offers limited security for your Azure resources only. Azure Defender tier extends these capabilities to on-premises and other clouds.

Main Functions of Microsoft Defender for Cloud

Cloud Security Posture Management (Available with Free Tier)

Microsoft Defender for Cloud continually assesses your resources, subscriptions, and organization for security issues. It then generates **Secure Score** and **Recommendations.**

Secure Score: The secure score is a measure of the security posture of your subscription: the higher the score, the lower the identified risk level. You can improve your secure score by remediating recommendations from your recommendations list.

Recommendations: Recommendations in Security Center detect threat against Azure Resources and displays them in Security Center Dashboard. By Remediating Recommendations you can reduce threat to your resources.

Cloud Workload Protection (Available with Paid Plans)

Cloud Workload Protection provides intelligent protection for your workloads. The Workload protections are provided through Microsoft Defender for Cloud **paid plans**. Table below shows partial list of features available with Azure/Microsoft Defender paid plans.

MS Defender for Servers	Vulnerability Assessment
MS Defender for Storage	Just-in-time VM access
MS Defender for SQL	Adaptive application control
MS Defender for App Services	File Integrity Monitoring
MS Defender for Key Vault	Network map
MS Defender for Azure Container Registry	

Exercise 15.4: Accessing Microsoft Defender for Cloud Dashboard

1. Open Chrome Browser and log on to Azure Portal @ portal.azure.com using Subscription Administrator credentials and password> Azure Portal opens as shown below. In Azure Portal Click 3 Horizontal lines in top left> A pane opens in left of Azure Portal as shown below> Note the **All services** option in left pane.

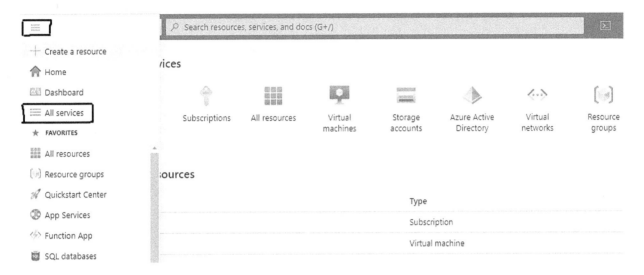

4. In Azure Portal Click All services in left pane> All Services pane opens as shown below> In All services pane scroll down in left pane till you see Security option > In right pane note the Microsoft Defender for Cloud option.

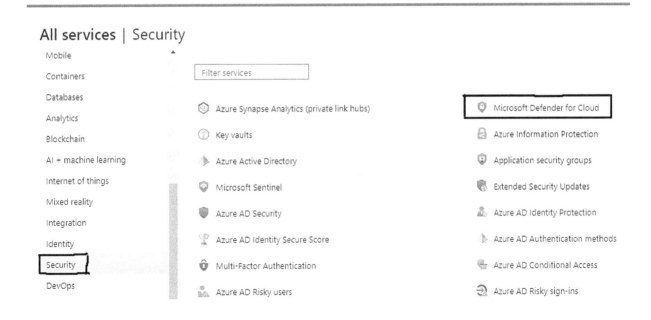

5. In above click Microsoft Defender for Cloud in right pane> Microsoft Defender for Cloud dashboard opens as shown below.

6. Scroll down in right pane and you can see Upgrade option> In next exercise we will upgrade Microsoft Defender for Cloud to Paid Tier.

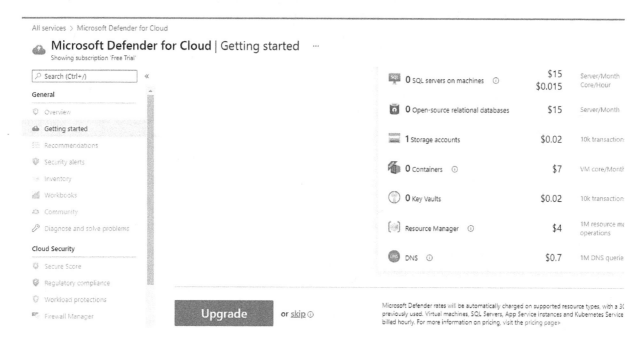

Exercise 15.5: Upgrade Microsoft Defender for Cloud to Paid Tier

1. Go to Microsoft Defender for Cloud dashboard and Scroll down in right pane> In right pane click Upgrade> Getting started pane opens as shown below> System will give you the option to install Log Analytics Agent in Virtual Machines. We will use this option.

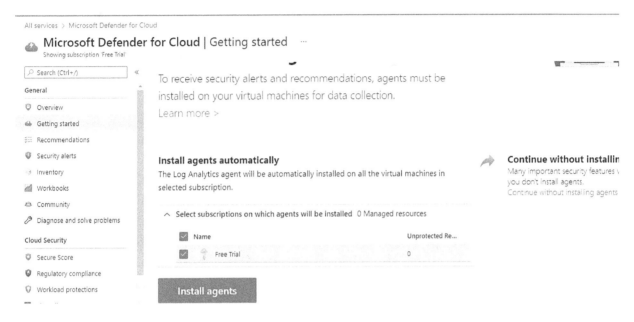

2. In above figure Click Install agents> Log Analytics Agent installation will be initiated in VMs> Microsoft Defender for Cloud paid tier dashboard opens as shown below> You can see all options in left pane are now active.

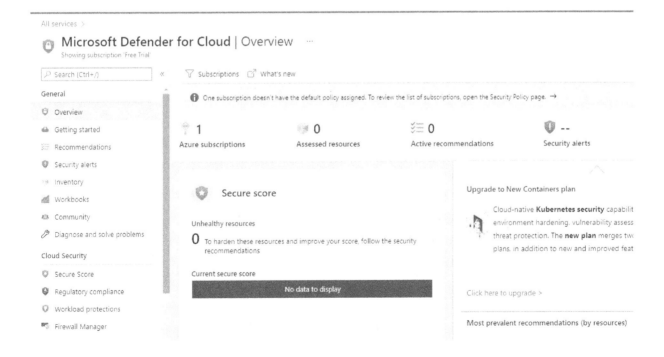

3. You need to wait till Log Analytics Agents are installed. I went to next step after 30-45 Minutes.

4. Go Virtual Machine vmcloud1 dashboard and click Extensions and applications in left pane> In right pane you can see Microsoft Monitoring Agent status is showing Provisioning succeeded. If required Click Refresh.

5. Similarly go Virtual Machine vmcloud2 dashboard and click Extensions and applications in left pane> In right pane you can see Microsoft Monitoring Agent status is showing Provisioning succeeded. If required Click Refresh.

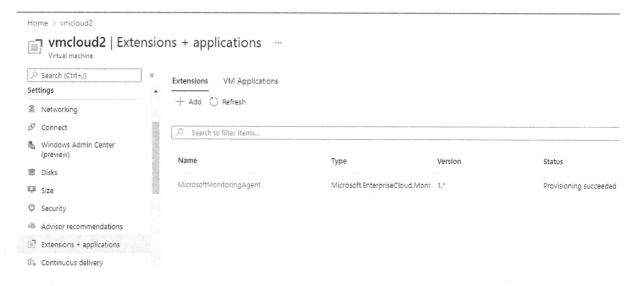

6. Wait for 12 hours or overnight before you proceed to next exercise. Make sure that VMs vmcloud1 and vmcloud2 are in Start mode. Don't stop them.

Exercise 15.6: Give Tenant wide access to Microsoft Defender for Cloud

In this Exercise we will give Tenant wide access to Microsoft Defender for Cloud to Subscription Administrator Singh Kohli. In Book Readers case it will be the name with which they signed for Azure Trial Subscription.

1. In Microsoft Defender for Cloud click Recommendations in left pane> In right pane note the link in top: **You may be viewing limited information. To get tenant-wide visibility, click here.**

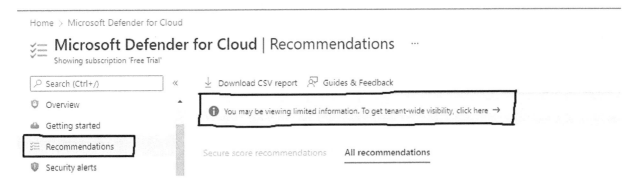

2. In above figure click link in top: **You may be viewing limited information. To get tenant-wide visibility, click here**> Tenant level Permissions pane opens as shown below> In Desired role select Security Admin> Click Get access.

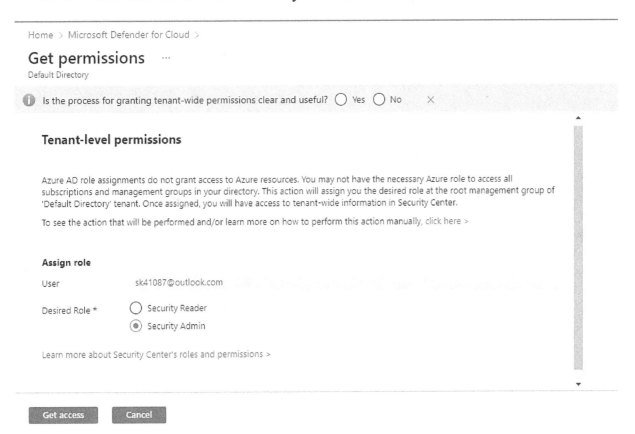

Azure Study & Lab Guide For Beginners

3. Following pane will open after you get notification that Permission is granted.

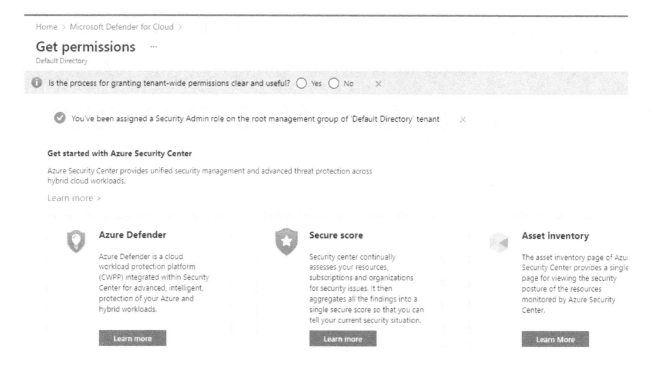

4. Close the Get permissions pane> You will be back in Microsoft Defender for Cloud dashboard with Recommendation selected in left pane> Refresh the page by pressing F5 on your laptop.

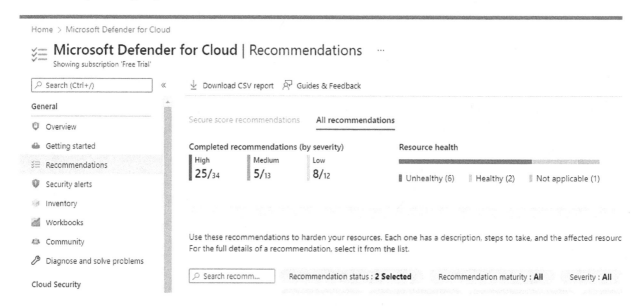

Recommendations

Recommendations are threat to your Azure resources. You need to remediate Recommendations to reduce threats to your Azure resources.

In other words Microsoft Defender for Cloud detects threat against Azure Resources and displays them in Recommendations pane.

By Remediating Recommendations you can reduce threat to your Azure resources.

Exercise 15.7: Detecting Threats using Recommendations

Microsoft Defender for Cloud Dashboard detects threats against Azure and Non-Azure resources and shows those threats in Recommendation dashboard as shown below.

Detecting Threats using Recommendations

1. Go to Microsoft Defender for Cloud Dashboard and click Recommendations in left pane> In right pane scroll down and you can see Recommendations generated by Microsoft Defender for Cloud. Scroll down to see more Recommendations.

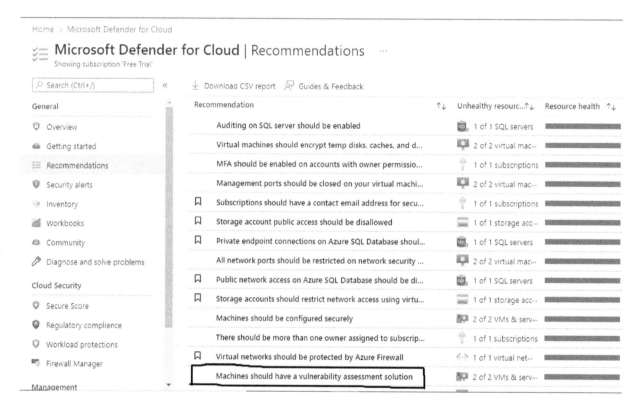

2. <u>You need to Remediate these Recommendation to improve your Security Posture.</u>

3. Note the Recommendation (Last Row in above figure) Machines should have a vulnerability assessment solution. In upcoming Exercise we will remediate this Recommendation.

Vulnerability Assessment Solutions for Virtual Machines

Vulnerability Assessment solution scans the VMs to detect and identify system and application vulnerabilities.

Currently, vulnerability assessment solutions are available from Microsoft Defender for Endpoint, Qualys and Rapid7 only.

Qualys Vulnerability Assessment solution

Qualys vulnerability scanner is included with Azure Security Center Defender Tier at no extra cost. To operate Qualys Vulnerability Assessment solution you don't need a Qualys license or even a Qualys account.

Using Azure Defender Dashboard you deploy Qualys extension on selected Azure VMs. The extension collects artifacts and sends them for analysis in the Qualys cloud service in the defined region. Qualys' cloud service conducts the vulnerability assessment and sends its findings to Security Center.

Figure below shows the Architecture of Qualys Vulnerability Assessment Solution.

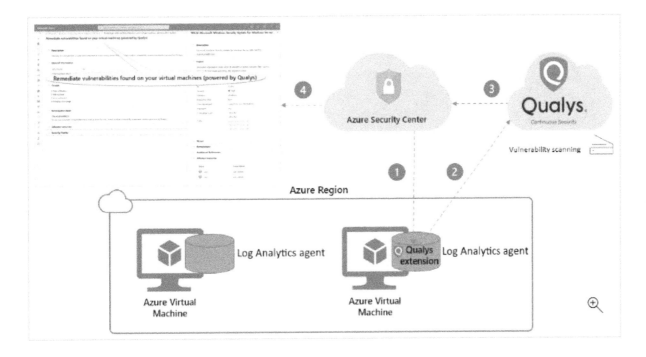

Exercise 15.8: Vulnerability Assessment of Servers (Azure VMs)

In this exercise we will install Qualys Vulnerability Extension on VMs: vmcloud1 and vmcloud2. VMs vmcloud1 and vmcloud2 were created in in Chapter 6. Make sure VMs vmcloud1 and vmcloud2 are started before you start Exercise in this Chapter.

1. Go to Microsoft Defender for Cloud Dashboard and click Recommendations in left pane> In right pane scroll down and you can see Recommendations generated by Microsoft Defender for Cloud> Note the Recommendation Machines should have a vulnerability solution.

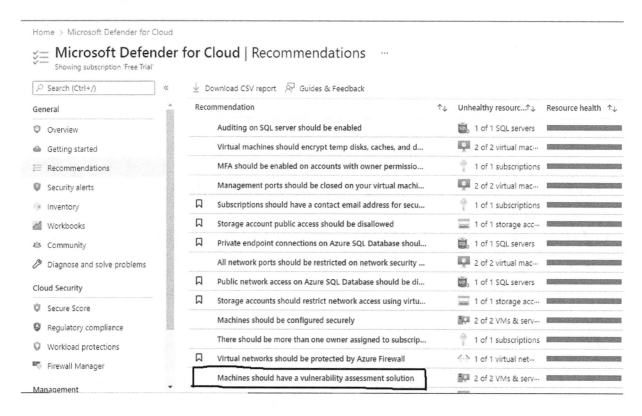

2. In above figure click row containing option Machines should have a vulnerability solution> Vulnerability assessment solution pane opens as shown below> scroll down and Select VMs: vmcloud1 and vmcloud2.

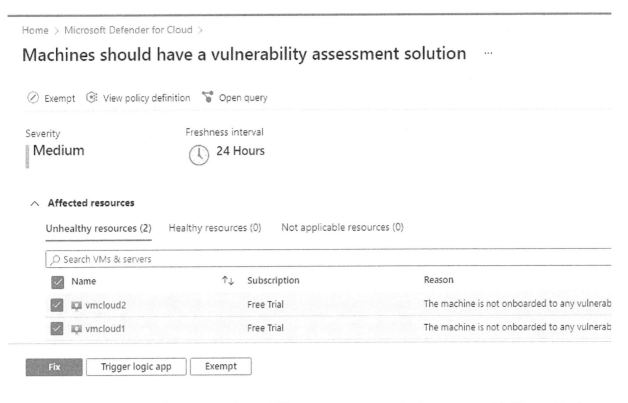

3. Click Fix in above figure> Vulnerability assessment solution pane with Remediation option opens as shown below> Make sure to select option **Deploy integrated vulnerability scanner powered by Qualys (included with Azure Defender for servers).**

Home > Microsoft Defender for Cloud > Machines should have a vulnerability assessment solution >

A vulnerability assessment solution should be enabled on your virt
Fixing vmcloud1, vmcloud2

Choose a vulnerability assessment solution:

◯ Threat and vulnerability management by Microsoft Defender for Endpoint (included with Microsoft Defender for servers)

◉ Deploy the integrated vulnerability scanner powered by Qualys (included with Microsoft Defender for servers)

◯ Deploy your configured third-party vulnerability scanner (BYOL - requires a separate license)

◯ Configure a new third-party vulnerability scanner (BYOL - requires a separate license)

Proceed

4. Click Proceed in above figure>Fixing Resource blade opens as shown below> Click Fix 2 Resources.

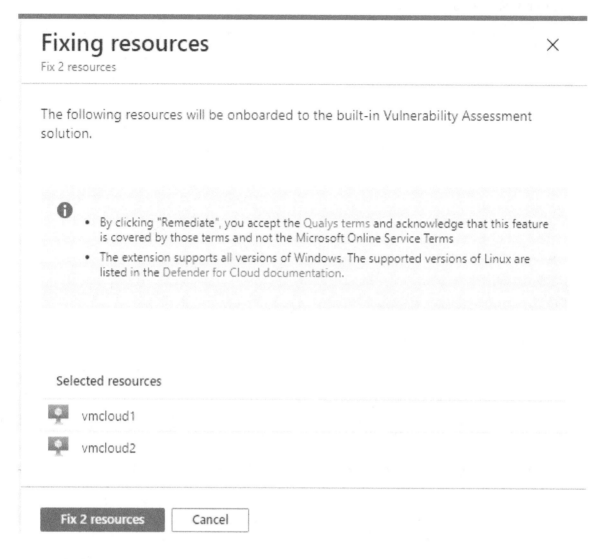

5. Wait for the Notification of success for Remediation. <u>Close the Vulnerability assessment solution pane after you receive notification of success.</u>
   Note: It may take up to 2-4 Hours until your resources move to the healthy resources tab.

6. We will come back to Vulnerability assessment solution pane after 2-4 Hours.

7. Close the Step 2 Figure pane.

8. This step I after did 2-4 Hours of Step 4. Go to Microsoft Defender for Cloud Dashboard and click Workloads protections in left pane> In right pane scroll down and you can see VM vulnerability assessment.

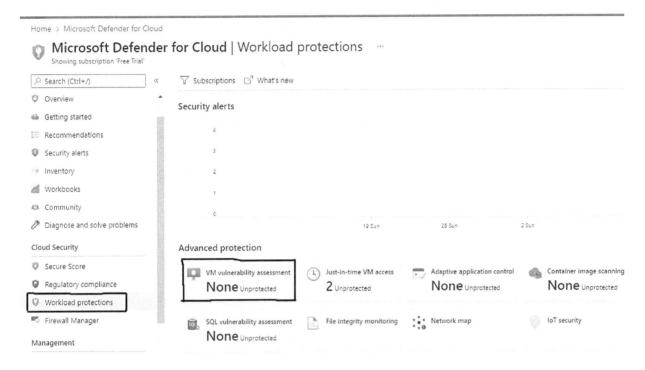

9. In above figure click VM vulnerability assessment> Machines should have a vulnerability assessment solution pane opens as shown below> Scroll down an dclick Healthy resources tab and you can see that Vulnerability solution is installed on both the VMs.

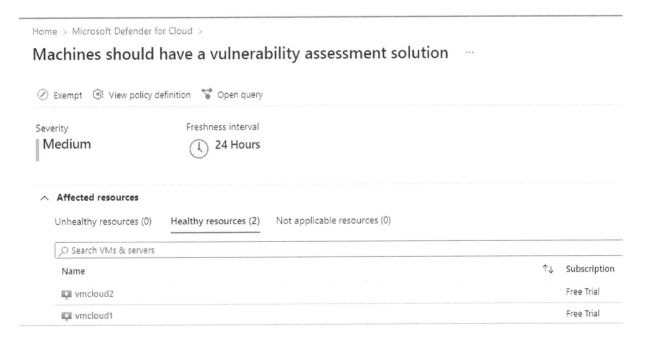

Result of above Configurations

After this Qualys Extension will perform vulnerabilty scan on VMs vmcloud1 and vmcloud2 to discover potential vulnerabilities in VMs.

10. Scroll up in above figure and you can see in below figure that a new Recommendation which says **Machines should have vulnerability findings resolved.** This recommendation has appeared because Qualys scanner performed vulnerabilty scan on VMs vmcloud1 and vmcloud2 and discovered potential vulnerabilities in VMs.

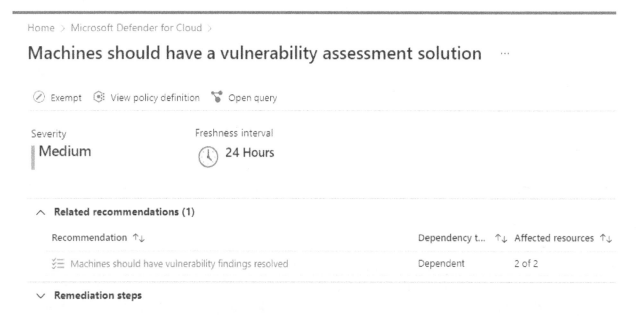

11. In above figure click link **Machines should have vulnerability findings resolved**> Machines should have vulnerability findings resolved pane appears as shown below> Scroll down and you can see potential vulnerabilities discovered by Qualys scanner.

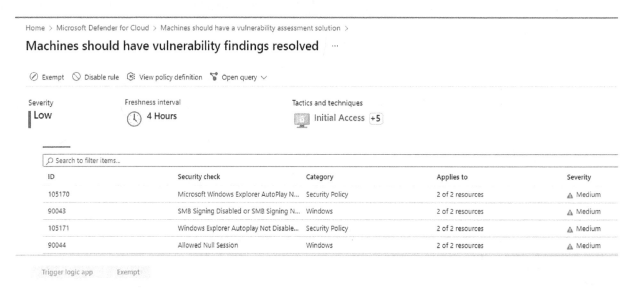